C000178890

HAUNTED
ESSEX

HAUNTED
ESSEX

CARMEL KING

The
History
Press

First published 2009

The History Press
The Mill, Brimscombe Port
Stroud, Gloucestershire, GL5 2QG
www.thehistorypress.co.uk

© Carmel King, 2009

The right of Carmel King to be identified as the Author
of this work has been asserted in accordance with the
Copyrights, Designs and Patents Act 1988.

All rights reserved. No part of this book may be reprinted
or reproduced or utilised in any form or by any electronic,
mechanical or other means, now known or hereafter invented,
including photocopying and recording, or in any information
storage or retrieval system, without the permission in writing
from the Publishers.
British Library Cataloguing in Publication Data.
A catalogue record for this book is available from the British Library.

ISBN 978 0 7524 5126 8

Typesetting and origination by The History Press
Printed in Great Britain

CONTENTS

ACKNOWLEDGEMENTS

I would like to thank the following people: first and foremost my daughter, Enya, for her love and enthusiasm for this project; Stephen King, for all his patience and assistance when I needed to visit and photograph some of the haunted places listed in this book; Anne-Marie O'Callaghan, for helping me track down stories; Lisa Mundy, for her help with the Running Well report; Janet Bord at Fortean Picture Library; the staff of the Kings Head at High Beach, Epping Forest, for their help; Bob Crump and all the staff and archaeologists at Foulness Heritage Centre; Tom Hodgeson, the Curator of Social History for Colchester Museums, and the staff at Hollytrees and East Lodge; Fleur at Stanstead Mountfitchet Castle; the staff at Coggeshall Heritage Centre; Thurrock Paranormal Team; Essex Paranormal Team. Also, a big thank you to Madison, Matt, Zak and the Leggett family, for all their love and support.

I would also like to thank my family, the O'Callaghans and the Trindles, for helping me whenever needed. My beloved parents, Rita and Tom, and my siblings, Rita, Brendan, Janice, Ursula, Tomas and Anne-Marie. The O'Callaghans and the Trindles always have a spooky story to tell!

Last but not least I wish to thank my friends for inspiring me and motivating me to meet my goals in life. You know who you are!

INTRODUCTION

Essex has been host to not only Britain's most infamous witch-hunt, but also, allegedly, the 'most haunted house in England' and one of the country's oldest reported ghosts! Matthew Hopkins' reign of terror and the bizarre hauntings of Borley Rectory have placed Essex firmly on the world's paranormal map. St Osyth from the seventh century is one of Britain's oldest reported ghosts; the oldest is in Hampshire, believed to be from that of a Bronze-Age man who rides a ghostly stallion that gallops across Bottlebrush Down.

Essex is labelled 'The Witch County' and an Essex ghost book would not be complete without stories of phantom witches and strange witchcraft-related tales. Hundreds of men, women and children were affected by the Essex Witch Trials in the sixteenth and seventeenth centuries. Villages were thrown into a chaos of fear, hatred and suspicion. The hysteria surrounding these events seems to have imprinted certain individuals to be replayed back to us as tortured wraiths through time.

The existence of ghosts remains a mystery and there is a group of experts constantly working to understand them and to prove whether or not they exist. Until that time, books, television programmes and stories will be dedicated to giving people the chills and making them wonder. The current theories on the existence of ghosts are as follows:

- Ghosts are the souls of the dead that have been unable to move on
- Ghosts are the souls of the dead that choose to haunt us, or are trying to send us a message
- Ghosts are a figment of people's imaginations and are fuelled by hysteria and hearsay
- Ghosts are a 'recording of time' just like a video tape, caused by certain conditions, such as four stone walls and the presence of electro-magnetic energy

Until these theories can be either proved or ruled out, we will forever be chilled by fireside tales or will dismiss them as fantasy. I will let you decide for yourself what you think of each tale and understand them as you choose. Either way, they are compelling insights into how people react to the unknown and how the human trait of hysteria can override people's imaginations. I have also added any claims of faking paranormal activity on once prominent ghost tales.

Tales of legendary folk such as Dick Turpin have had their legacy extended further when their ghosts have allegedly been spotted in their old 'hunting-grounds' across Essex. I started this book with the intention of tracking down every on-going haunting that I possibly could and hopefully I have succeeded, give or take a few!

Sleep tight!

Carmel King, 2009

one

HAUNTED HOUSES

Borley Rectory

I felt that 'the most haunted house in England' deserved its place at the very beginning of this journey through haunted Essex. Borley Rectory burned down in 1939 and although the site remains empty to this day, the village still attracts unwanted attention all these years later. Borley is no longer haunted and the locals are tired of all and sundry descending on their village in search of ghosts that they say ceased to exist as soon as the rectory was demolished.

One man claims to have faked the Borley hauntings, but this has been disputed by many people due to the very early sightings of the 'Borley Nun', and the great length of time the hauntings continued. Also, by his own admission, he recalled events that he could not explain and which he did not fake.

The rectory's story begins in 1863, when the Revd Henry Bull had the oversized rectory built to house his family, which was outgrowing Borley Place. The rectory was constructed opposite the parish church, on ground where there had been sightings of a spectral nun, floating mournfully across the plot of land. Builders asked Revd Bull if he had heard the tales of the nun and asked if he was sure that he wanted building to go ahead, but the reverend laughed off their tales and gave details of how he wanted the sprawling twenty-five-roomed rectory to look. In 1863, the building was complete and the Bull family moved in. The house had a dead stillness inside, accompanied by an everlasting chill, even during the summertime. Such a large house was bound to have creaks, groans and knocks, but not Borley Rectory: the house remained silent throughout and when unexplained things did happen, they were all the more terrifying. The only thing that made noise of its own accord was the water pump: a large clumsy contraption that made odd clanks and gasps. When the strange events in the house began the family were sure to rule out the pump as the cause of the noises before investigating further.

The first unexplained incident was witnessed by two of the Bull daughters and their nursemaid. The trio were standing in the drive when the girls noticed a pair of friends crossing some nearby fields. The friends were accompanied by a woman in white who neither of the girls recognised as a local. They thought nothing more until they met the girls and questioned them about their female companion. However, neither girl had any idea what the Bull daughters meant; they insisted they were alone in the fields.

The next phenomenon was the incessant ringing of the servants' bells, to the extent that the wires to the bells were cut in an attempt to silence them. But they continued to ring. It was first thought that mice were to blame, but with the wires to the bells cut, how could they have rung? Ethel Bull was witness to this event when alone in the rectory one afternoon. She said every bell rang and she ran to find the cause of the ringing to try and silence them. At this point the distinct sound of rushing water was heard; this was most peculiar as the house had no plumbing!

The next and most famous episode of the Borley hauntings now began. One evening as the Bull family sat down to dinner and chatted happily, the temperature in the dining room suddenly dropped. The chatting stopped and one of the girls gasped and pointed at the side window. There stood a nun; staring sadly in at the family before turning and walking out of view. This happened many times; each time Revd Henry Bull and his sons would run outside to talk to the nun but she would already have vanished. It was impossible that she could have run and hid in just a few seconds. Fed up with this frequent occurrence, the reverend ordered that the window be bricked up. It was believed that the rectory had been built across the Nun's haunting path and the Revd Bull was so taken by the spectre that he had an octagonal summer house built opposite what came to be known as the Nun's Walk. She would manifest in the far corner of the garden before drifting along the 'Walk' and disappearing out of view.

Borley Rectory, 12 June 1929. (Reproduced with kind permission from Fortean Picture Library)

Borley Rectory's gates, where the nun was sighted on a few occasions. (Reproduced with kind permission from Fortean Picture Library)

Now the poltergeist activity began. One of the Bull daughters was sleeping alone in her room when she was awoken by having her face slapped. Over a period of time, this activity escalated and each night upon retiring to bed she would hear loud rapping sounds on the bedroom door and the entire family would hear multiple bangs and crashes throughout the house. When the sounds were investigated, all was still, as before. Then the heavy, purposeful footsteps, that would echo through the house, began. At 10.30 p.m. every night, the Bull girls would hear the footsteps coming up the corridor, walk past their door and stop outside the night nursery. Three taps would be heard and then silence once more, unless the crashing sounds began. Some guests who were invited to stay at the rectory would leave hurriedly the next day, refusing to stay another moment. Strange lights would illuminate rooms and could be seen from outside and from under closed doors. Upon investigation, the rooms would be in darkness. Electricity was not wired into Borley Rectory and it was lit entirely by oil lamps; this discounts the possibility of faulty wiring or switches.

The next occurrences were witnessed by P. Shaw Jeffrey, an old student friend of Harry Bull Jnr, who had also attended Wadam College, Oxford. Shaw Jeffrey was a teacher (later a headmaster) and spent the summer holidays at Borley Rectory as a guest. He recalled stones flying about inside the house, the sighting of a nun and regularly heard the sound of a horse-drawn carriage, with no explanation. His boots were also moved from his bedpost to the top of the wardrobe. Then his dictionary vanished, and he was awoken by a loud bang and found the dictionary on the floor in the middle of the room.

Servants and maids then began to have terrifying experiences and left the rectory hastily. One woman was frightened by the footsteps in the corridor that stopped outside her room. Others were scared witless by a horse-drawn carriage that would fly through the dining room wall and out across the garden, before vanishing into thin air. Members of the public had now begun hearing disembodied footsteps outside the rectory and the first apparitions began. Ethel Bull saw a dark-skinned man in one of the upstairs corridors and later saw another 'strange looking' man standing by her bed. She was not the only person to see this man, as other family members, guests and staff began seeing him too.

In 1892, the first chapter in Borley Rectory's history came to a close as Revd Henry Bull died in the Blue Room of the rectory after an illness, aged only 59, and his son Harry succeeded him as Rector and head of the house. Henry Bull was not the first person to suffer from ill health or an untimely death at the rectory.

Next came the most poignant sighting of the nun. On 28 July 1900, Mabel and Freda Bull were returning from a summer party and approached the rectory via a gateway near a copse at the back of the grounds. As they came through the trees, there stood the nun. Her head was bent and the girls froze momentarily, noting the agony etched on the nun's face. Freda is said to have run into the house and fetched the eldest Bull daughter, Dodie (Elizabeth). Dodie scoffed at the suggestion of a ghost and stormed out of the rectory to confront the mysterious nun on the lawn. The three Bull girls watched the nun literally 'drift' across the path, before turning to look directly at them and then vanish.

A carpenter named Fred Cartwright was the next to see the nun, standing on the driveway. He saw her again in the same place four days later, her eyes closed and face forlorn. He wanted to speak to her, but walked on. He momentarily paused and turned to her and she had vanished into thin air. He saw her again the following morning, but as he approached to speak to her, she vanished in front of his eyes!

The final saga of the Bull family residence was the strange occurrences reported by Mr and Mrs Edward Cooper, employees of the Bulls, who resided in the stable cottage. Strange noises would keep the couple awake at night; numerous sightings of the nun and the vision of the phantom coach were among the paranormal things reported by the hard-headed couple. In 1927 Harry Bull died of cancer aged 62 in the Blue Room, like his father before him and another era came to an end. Many people came to view the rectory in order to take up the post as rector, but left hastily, with a definite 'No!' to the job.

Over a year later, in the autumn of 1928, Revd Guy Smith and his wife Mabel accepted the post at Borley. Mabel decided to get on with spring cleaning the clumsy, dusty mansion without the aid of maids and found a box on a shelf in the library. When she opened it she reeled in horror, as the contents of the box proved to be a human skull, later identified by a doctor as female. The Smiths then began to experience the rectory's phenomena. Revd Smith was alone in the house one day when he clearly heard mumbling coming from the Blue Room. As he approached, the volume of the voice increased and he clearly heard a woman cry out, 'No Carlos, don't!' and the voice faded away. The couple heared the footsteps in the corridor outside their room, so Revd Smith decided to hide in the corridor with a hockey stick. He jumped out to confront the intruder, but suddenly realised he was alone in the corridor!

Borley Rectory, 17 August 1943. (Reproduced with kind permission from Fortean Picture Library)

The infamous 'floating brick' photograph. A brick can be seen apparently in mid-air in the doorway to the right-centre of photograph. (Reproduced with kind permission from Fortean Picture Library)

Borley Church today. (Author's Collection)

Servants began to report seeing the phantom coach and Mable Smith saw a 'grey wispy figure' leaning against one of the gates, but when she approached, it vanished. The Smiths began to experience the same phenomena as the Bulls had, from the incessant bell ringing to the smashing of household objects. Revd Smith even contacted the *Daily Mirror* about the activity, to see if they could be of any help. The infamous Harry Price was sent to investigate. Price travelled up to Borley with his secretary and Mr V.C. Wall, a reporter, on 12 June 1929.

The first séance at the rectory took place that very night. The séance was held in the Blue Room and a planchette was used as the tool for the 'spirits' to contact the group. The spirit contacted was Revd Harry Bull, who claimed to be unhappy and that he had been murdered and had not died of cancer. During the séance, Price claimed to see Bull standing behind Revd Smith and the Smiths were so alarmed that they demanded the séance be stopped. They forbade any further séances while they were in residence. The newspaper wanted detailed reports from the house and the rectory's privacy was blown away. Nine months later, not long after the investigations began, the Smiths quit Borley Rectory. Mable had been constantly unwell and the huge, cold rectory was depressing the couple. Harry Price had to cease the investigations while the house lay empty, but local villagers began to report bizarre goings on at the empty rectory, including furniture being hurled about. The final straw for the Smiths was on the 18 March 1930, when they approached the house to check on their stored furniture and heard what they described as, 'the most horrible sounds coming from the house'. By April, the couple had left Borley for good.

On 16 October 1930, a new rector and his family arrived in Borley: the Revd Lionel Algernon Foyster, his very young wife, Marianne and their adopted daughter Adelaide. Revd Foyster was a cousin of the Bull family and this chapter in the rectory's history would be by far the most violent and turbulent of all. The ghosts didn't wait long to begin tormenting the family, as on the first day Marianne distinctly heard her name being called, although she was alone in the house. This was followed by numerous people hearing the disembodied footsteps, Marianne seeing the apparition of Harry Bull, poltergeist activity, perfume smells, the bell ringing, and the disappearance of inanimate objects. On 25 February 1930, all the objects that had disappeared were found piled up in the kitchen and the next day a pile of old books appeared under their bed. That evening of the 26th, Marianne was walking past the Blue Room with a candle in hand when she was struck violently across the face, so violently that the skin beneath her eye broke and the eye blackened. The very next night at bedtime, the couple were attacked by a flying cotton reel and the head of a hammer. Both objects flitted about before crashing to the ground.

On the 28 February, Revd Foyster was in his study when he got up to leave the room. He returned moments later to find two of the chairs littered with upright pins! Shortly afterwards he tripped over a saucepan and oil lamp which were on the floor outside his room and he found a polisher handle a little further up the corridor, as if left to hurt him. On 5 March he was hit by a hairbrush and Marianne had a doorknob thrown at her. Their nephew, Richard, had been at the rectory, witnessed violent paranormal activity and saw that Marianne, who was unwell, had been physically attacked and thrown from her bed. On Monday 8 June, Marianne retreated to Arthur Hall in Sudbury, owned by Sir and Lady Whitehouse. She remained at the Hall for many weeks and the Revd Foyster refused to sleep alone in the rectory. Sir and Lady Whitehouse had also witnessed activity for themselves at the rectory, including the wood panelling in the upstairs of the house being set alight.

On 13 October 1930 Harry Price and his Council for Psychic Research were invited to the rectory for a meeting with Revd Foyster. The party had brought two bottles of wine to contribute to the refreshments and when the red wine was poured it turned to ink, although the rest of the bottle was perfect. The white wine, upon pouring, smelt of strong perfume, while the rest of that bottle also remained perfect. The servants' bells also decided to begin one of their manic ringing sessions.

After the meeting, the party retired to their hotel and began discussing the evening's events. Harry Price pointed the finger at Marianne as the most likely suspect to be faking the activity. This damaged the investigation and Revd Foyster banned Price from the rectory until Sidney Glanville, a draughtsman and professional engineer, helped the pair patch their differences after making Price see that it couldn't possibly have been Marianne. Further investigations saw the appearance of messages on walls saying 'Marianne please help get' and 'Get light mass prayers'. In the October of 1935, events and ill health had taken their toll on the Foyster's, notably that of the reverend who had become crippled by arthritis, and they vacated the rectory, leaving it uninhabited for eighteen months.

After the Foyster's departure, the Church of England decided to merge the village's parish with the one at nearby Liston and put the rectory up for sale. Harry Price jumped at the chance and offered the church rent money while they waited for a sale. The church found this offer too good to refuse and it gave Price the valuable opportunity to investigate the property as he saw fit. His first act was to assemble a team of professional, level-headed sceptics by posting an advertisement in *The Times*. From this he found forty-eight trustworthy people who ranged from Oxford undergraduates and officers in the RAF to doctors and BBC Television engineers. Price laid down a set of strict rules and pointers for carrying out

The 'Marianne Writings' found after séances. (Reproduced with kind permission Fortean Picture Library)

successful, foolproof investigations. Much activity was recorded by Price's team, including the movement of objects and contact with the spirits via countless séances. This included one from a mysterious woman called Marie Lairre, a woman murdered in the 1600s; could this have been the Borley Nun?

Price and his team left residence of the rectory in 1939, after it was purchased by a retired Captain of the Royal Engineers; Captain William Hart Gregson. Gregson renamed the rectory 'The Priory' and set about getting the place insured for £10,000. Ten weeks later, Gregson was sorting out piles of his precious books when an oil lamp 'mysteriously' overturned and started a fire. The fire brigade arrived too late to save the structure and the flames weren't put out until the roof had burned away and all inside was wrecked. A group of onlookers reported seeing a young girl dressed in blue in the window of the Blue Room as flames licked around the window frames. That was the end of the rectory and although activity was reported in the ruins, all activity ceased after the complete demolition in the late 1940s.

Borley Church has also been the site of alleged paranormal activity, but it is widely believed to just be wishful thinking.

Mucking Hall, Mucking

The entire village of Mucking is now owned by a private firm and all buildings in the vicinity are used as offices. Mucking Hall was the prominent landmark of the village, but it sadly burned down a few years ago. Up until the fire, people reported seeing a ghostly face in one of the windows of the empty hall. The ghost of a smuggler, who was hanged from a large tree near the church gates, is said to haunt the road from the church to the village pub.

The 'Lady of the Lake' is the ghostly form of a woman seen walking from the village pond back towards Mucking Hall. She is believed to be the young girl who drowned herself after her parents disapproved of the man she loved and forbade them to marry, even after she fell pregnant with his child.

St Clere's Hall, Stanford le Hope

St Clere's Hall is now home to the local golf club, but in its 315-year history it has had many name changes, owners and ghostly occurrences. Once home to the Clerk for George I and George II's stables, it is rumoured that George I occasionally kept his lions in the cellars of St Clere's while passing up the River Thames!

Poltergeist activity has been reported in the main room downstairs; the back office has an uneasy feel and a ghostly female figure has been reported in the main room upstairs. There has also been a figure standing at a window in the loft and staff complain of a feeling they are being watched.

When a paranormal team were invited to do an investigation at the Hall they came away with some very interesting results. While the mediums picked up on

St Clere's Hall, Stanford-le-Hope. (Author's Collection)

St Clere's Hall, viewed from the south, Stanford-le-Hope. (Author's Collection)

numerous 'energies' in the building, definite temperature drops were noted by the team's equipment; in one case the temperature dropped from 22°C to 11°C before climbing to a sweltering 30°C and dropping back to 22°C again. The heating system was not switched on during the team's visit.

The most notable incident for the team was when one of the mediums was allegedly told by his 'spirit guide' that he was going to 'play' with the team's equipment! At that moment the EMF meter went off the scale and only dropped when the medium requested it. Even more fascinating was that the temperature notably dropped during that time. A video camera was also left running in a locked room for two hours and study of the footage showed nine separate light anomalies and three very bright sparks that flashed.

Layer Marney Tower, Layer Marney

Lord Marney unfortunately died before seeing the completion of his beautiful Layer Marney Tower. The tower is currently open to the public and many people have been scared witless by the ghost of Lord Marney, who reputedly charges down the staircase at speed!

Lord Marney is also said to haunt Layer Marney Church and is believed to be the owner of the disembodied voice that occasionally echoes through the church. The church is also host to a most bizarre ghost – that of a headless chicken, which is often seen running among the headstones!

Beeleigh Abbey, Maldon

The beautiful Beeleigh Abbey is said to by haunted by a previous owner, none other than Sir John Gates; a former High Sheriff of Essex who had bought the abbey in 1537 for around £300. The abbey was once home to Cistercian monks, untill Henry VIII's Dissolution of Monasteries. Sir John was later involved in a plot to put Lady Jane Grey on the throne and was beheaded at the Tower of London on 22 August 1553 for treason. His screams of anguish are said to echo through the abbey.

Other hauntings are confined to the James Room. People have had a great sense of being watched here, while a member of staff once reported seeing a hooded monk standing in the room. It is reported that one previous owner of the abbey decided to sleep in the James Room one night and was rudely awoken at 3 a.m. by an unseen force that shook her bed. The lady then experienced a pain in one of her arms, which required medical attention the next morning. The doctor could only describe the injury to the woman's arm as not unlike a bite from a tropical insect! A last chilling find in the abbey has only been recently unearthed. Two unidentified skeletons were found at the bottom of the pond in the abbey's grounds; could they have been two of the monks who were chased from the abbey by Tudor soldiers?

Layer Marney Tower. (Author's Collection)

Beeleigh Abbey. (Author's Collection)

The Tudor House, Maldon

This sixteenth-century house in a quieter part of Maldon has allegedly been haunted by a 'demon'. The house has a long history of complaints made by staff who left after being terrorised by a ghost. Two sisters once resided in the house before the younger sister stole her older sister's boyfriend and promptly married him! Over time, the sisters appeared to have settled their differences and the younger sister invited the older girl to come and stay with them. The older girl was quick to take the opportunity to kill her sister by suffocating her with a pillow. Her ghost has been seen in the window on numerous occasions, even when the house is empty. A passing priest once approached the house to speak with the mysterious woman in the window, but he felt some kind of force push him back down the driveway. Servants have had bedclothes ripped off in the night and been terrorised by loud bumps and crashes. It is said that one servant was chased by the lady who haunts the window and jumped to her death. Passers-by speak of a woman with grey straggly hair and 'the most wretched expression etched on her face.'

Ingatestone Hall, Ingatestone

In 1548, William Petre, who lived at after Ingatestone Manor, had Ingatestone Hall built. The hall boasts two famous ghosts. One is possibly Lady Katherine Grey, younger sister of Lady Jane Grey. Lady Katherine married the Earl of Hertford without first seeking consent from the Queen Elizabeth. She was put into th custody of Sir William Petre under the queen's orders for two years, of which most time was served at Ingatestone Hall.

The other ghost is that of Sir William himself! Sir William was one of the Royal Commissioners of the Dissolution of the Monasteries. Ingatestone Manor had belonged to the nuns of Barking Convent, before he purchased it from the Crown. He worked under Henry VIII, Edward VI and Mary I and managed to live through all the politics surrounding the suffering of the Catholics and Protestants and was host to Elizabeth I at Ingatestone in 1561.

Ridgemarsh Farm, Foulness Island

Ridgemarsh Farm is one of numerous 'creepy' houses on the island. A local archaeologist decided to conduct a house search with a lady who was a spiritual medium. When they reached Ridgemarsh Farm, the woman said she had a 'terrible feeling' and had to get out of the house. She visualised a lady in Edwardian dress and said that something terrible had happened in the house connected with the woman and two children. The archaeologist was stunned and had no idea what she was talking about. They later discovered that a lady who lived in Ridgemarsh Farm during the early twentieth century was devastated by the loss of her two babies; believed to have both been stillborn or to have died shortly after birth. Other locals also said that place gave them a terrible feeling.

Treasure Holt, Clacton-on-Sea

Treasure Holt is a bizarre home, host to a catalogue of strange and historical events. It was investigated by the Society of Physical Research during the 1920s, the BBC in 1970, and by the crew from *Most Haunted* in recent years. Treasure Holt, built on the isolated edge of Holland Marshes, dates back to long before 1138 and was a coaching inn for many years, named Perles Farm. One of the first reported hauntings here was the sighting of a lady in a 'crinoline dress'; exactly one year later the Crinoline Lady was seen again, this time floating across the lounge, before vanishing into thin air! On 26 December 1960, a boy living at Treasure Holt saw the ghost of his deceased father float through the front wall, dressed in his suit! The ghost walked towards the middle of the room, stopped and stared at the three people sitting there and turned to walk back through the wall he had just come through! He had died four years previously and the boy was the only one who saw him. A monk has also been repeatedly reported, floating 1ft above ground level, across the grounds. Percy, a blonde lady, is another ghost at Treasure Holt. She is a previous disgruntled homeowner who sits in the fireplace and is believed to be the same woman who rides up and down the lane on a phantom horse. Even the woodland outside the property does not escape the bizarre hauntings and the ghost of an executed highwayman still swings from the trees.

Thorn Hotel, Mistley

The row of houses next to the Thorn Hotel, Mistley, all boast their own ghost tales. One is of an old man who was cruelly left to die by his uncaring lodgers. His agonising cries have been heard coming from his old bedroom and many have reported seeing him walking around the first floor.

Saffron Walden

Hill House is in Saffron Walden's High Street. It is described as being haunted by a 'little ghost' that is responsible for causing sudden icy draughts in corridors. This is reputedly thought to be caused by a young maid called Nelly Ketteridge who used to work there. On 6 January 1845 Nelly made her way home to Elmdon, but was caught in a violent snowstorm. Her lifeless body was found in a ditch between Wendens Ambo and Wenden Loft. Servants at Hill House became accustomed to the activity and accepted the ghost as part of the building.

Perhaps Saffron Walden's best-loved haunted place is that of The Maltings, now used as a youth hostel. This 600-year-old building is by far the oldest inhabited building in Saffron Walden and ghost hunters are always most welcome to come and spend the night there. A woman is reported to have fallen through the floor to her death in an apparent DIY mishap, after her husband had lifted the floor and her shade is said to walk the corridors. Her presence could signal that she didn't die accidentally, but was deliberately murdered! Footsteps are said to be heard climbing an iron staircase, although the property has no such staircases. Unexplained noises, dark shadowy figures, ghostly children and doors that open and close by themselves are just some of the things ghost hunters can expect to encounter here. The most haunted part of the entire building is said to be the cellar.

Shoeburyness

Red House, in the town of Shoeburyness, was built in 1673 and is said to be haunted by the ghost of a girl who slit her own throat to spite her lover. Occupants of the house over the years have heard unexplained knocks and bangs and in 1948 a secret underground tunnel was discovered leading from the house to Shoebury Manor. This has now been filled in.

Shoebury Barracks are now no longer used by the army, but many years ago one of the barracks buildings caught fire and burned to the ground, killing several people. The buildings that replaced them are now believed to be haunted.

Thundersley

In the late 1940s there was a haunting at a house in Selbourne Road, Thundersley, that terrified the occupants, a mother and daughter, so much that it caused them to flee. They began to hear the sound of hobnail boots trampling towards the house. Over the next few months, the sound began to get louder and louder and scared them witless when it began to bang on the walls. Things came to a head when the ghost began randomly screaming and the occupants fled. It is thought that the father was killed during one of the World Wars; maybe it was his tortured soul that returned to his home in Thundersley.

Wheelers Cottage on Bread and Cheese Hill was built around 1700 as a thatched property. Mrs Wheel had many children, but two of her sons were killed in action during the Crimean War. She mourned her sons and in some sort of attempt to contact their spirits, blew on a trumpet or bugle in the early hours of the morning. She was known to be a white witch and a holy woman and longed to contact her dead sons. A family living there in the late 1900s was awoken at around 3 a.m. one morning by the sound of a bugle. This continued every new moon until more recent years. The family did not know anything about the lady who had lost her sons in the war until they were told afterwards. Nowadays, the property has been an Indian takeaway for many years.

South Benfleet

A family living in a house near Cemetery Corner from the 1960s to the late 1990s experienced much paranormal activity over the years. A friend of the family witnessed activity from 1989 to 1997 and recorded a catalogue of events that took place within the chalet-style house. The people living in the house during this period were middle-aged parents and two of their sons; one in his late teens and early twenties the other in his late twenties. They also had two daughters in their mid-twenties who lived nearby. While in an upstairs room at the back of the property, early one Sunday morning, the younger brother and his girlfriend became aware of someone standing in the doorway. When they turned to look, the coats on the door were left swinging. They both ran out to confront the intruder, but the house was empty.

On another occasion, the couple decided to take the washing in from the garden and both distinctly heard the microwave bell ring. Not only was the microwave not in use by either of them, but it was also unplugged from the wall! It was at this moment that loud bangs were heard on the floor above them, the room they had been in earlier. They rushed up the stairs to see who was there, but all was in order and no one was in the house. The final thing to happen that morning was the very loud clattering of cutlery coming from the kitchen, but again all proved to be in order.

The family cat would also behave strangely at times, rearing up and hissing at an invisible intruder. Strange smells would be noted in particular areas around the house, notably that of fresh onions, but on one occasion in the summertime it was of Christmas pudding! Light switches would be flicked up and down and television sets would mysteriously switch on, even when switched off by the main button!

One evening things took a strange turn for the family; the youngest son and daughter, along with their friend, went up to the master bedroom with the intention of telephoning their eldest sister, who lived nearby with her two young daughters. As the brother and sister chatted briefly, a large heavy photograph album lifted off the top shelf and flew a distance of about 6ft, striking the brother before landing open upon the bed. The page showed a photograph of the two young nieces and at that moment the telephone rang and one of the nieces was on the other end of the line!

The last phenomenon witnessed in the house followed a family dispute. The parents and the youngest son were the only people living in the property at this time and the son's girlfriend was staying for the weekend. As arguments flared the girl became a little upset and retired to bed. After a short while her boyfriend joined her, but he fell asleep fairly quickly. After a few moments the girl noticed smoke near the curtains and instantly thinking her boyfriend hadn't extinguished his cigarette properly, sat up to put it out, but as she sat up, she remembered he didn't have a cigarette before going to bed. She sat there for a moment looking at the smoke before realising that it was very still, not swirling or rising in any way. In front of her eyes, the centre of the 'cloud' moved and formed a face, the face of an elderly gentleman with his eyes closed. This then slowly moved toward her and passed by, exiting out of the bedroom door before vanishing! The next morning when she told the family what she had seen, two of them recalled being terrified by a man in a cloak that one day had appeared at that very same window when they were little children!

Bradwell-on-Sea

Linnets Cottage in Bradwell-on-Sea stands close to where Othona Fort used to be and is now used by the RSPB as accommodation for bird watchers, as the nearby estuary of the River Blackwater attracts hundreds of ducks, geese and rare birds. The cottage used to be home to Walter Linnet in the early 1900s. Walter Linnet was the finest gun punter in the area and made a living from shooting ducks. People staying the night at Linnets Cottage have told of how they woke in the night to find a man standing at the foot of the bed, staring at them. Others tell of seeing a man peering in the cottage windows. All descriptions fit that of Walter Linnet!

Bradwell Lodge in Bradwell-Juxta-Mare was once the village rectory. A man and child are said to haunt this building and although no identity can be traced for the child, the man is believed to have been the butler to the Rector of Bradwell. The butler had attempted to commit suicide in one of the first-floor rooms. His initial attempt failed. However, whatever he had done to kill himself worked slowly and he died as he reached the ground floor. His ghost is seen exiting one of the upstairs rooms and vanishing down the stairs. One maid slept for a night in the room where the butler had attempted suicide, but refused to stay there any longer. She did not explain why and appeared to be terrified out of her wits!

Kelvedon Hall, Kelvedon

Kelvedon Hall and the nearby churchyard are said to be haunted by phantom hounds: one was shot on the church altar by a disgruntled landowner and the other was a favourite pet that had passed away.

Chingford Hall, Chingford

Chingford Hall was host to an unknown entity that would strike in pitch darkness. Some years ago, a wandering tramp spent the night at the hall. He was found to be insane the following day and admitted to a mental hospital.

Coggeshall

Coggeshall Abbey had a bizarre kind of haunting between the years 1176 and 1194. A crowd of Knights Templars were spotted chatting in the guesthouse and the hostler arranged for the Knights to be accommodated. Upon his return to the guesthouse, the knights had vanished and no one could account for who they were. They were spotted a few times after this initial event.

Cradle House, near Markshall Old Rectory, used to be the secret meeting place for the monks from Coggeshall Abbey. The monks have been seen in spirit form, retracing their steps from the abbey to Cradle House. Witnesses of this eerie, floating procession describe how the monks are all hooded and wearing white robes.

Guild House in Market End has the ghost of an elderly man that has been seen by many visitors, standing at the foot of a bed in one of the bedrooms. Unexplained lights have been noted in the attic room by people passing by.

In Church Street, a secret room was discovered in one of the houses and ever since it was opened up, poltergeist activity has occurred throughout the building and visitors have noticed a strange presence.

Dedham

A cottage in Brook Street is haunted by a little boy who suffocated while sweeping the chimney. Children report seeing a very real boy with a blackened, dirty face who wants to play, only to scare them witless as they try to grab him and have their hands pass right through!

Loughton

Three-hundred-year-old Woolston Hall is sat in the middle of Woolston Manor Golf Course. In 1980 contractors were working on the hall, carrying out a £100,000 refit; but strange disturbances began to cause workmen to down tools and then there was a total refusal to even enter the third floor. A psychic researcher led an investigation and found that a 13-year-old girl called Agnes committed suicide here over 200 years ago, by jumping out of a third-floor window. The alterations to the Hall seemed to have upset the balance and workmen reported many strange phenomena, including severe temperature drops, shuffling sounds, breaking glass, and mysterious knocks and bangs. Even more bizarre was that the spirit tended only to target men!

Loughton Hall on Rectory Lane is haunted by a tormented wraith known as 'Mary'. She froze to death in the Hall grounds and now locks doors from the inside of rooms, forcing the caretaker to have to call a locksmith every time. Her ghost has been seen standing on the first-floor landing, looking down the stairs. Two male ghosts have also been seen in the Hall: a man dressed in black and another dressed in tweeds. In 2000 some people saw the ghost of a soldier in a small patch of woodland near the Hall.

Alderton Hall is home to the tragic ghost of a maid who was thrown out of the Hall after she gave birth to the child of the Master of the Hall. She drowned the baby in the pond before killing herself; she is said to haunt the upper floors of the hall. A blonde male ghost dressed in a red cloak has been seen on the driveway, but his identity is unsure. A piano is also heard being played in the Hall.

Epping

Beech House is haunted by Sir Francis, who fell in love with Lady Elizabeth, daughter of the Lord of Beech House. Elizabeth's father disliked Sir Francis and had him turned over to the enemy. Sir Francis has been seen looking out of the windows on the upper floor of the house, while Lady Elizabeth and her father haunt other parts of the building.

A private house in Oakwood Hill is haunted by an unseen entity that pushes people down the stairs, often resulting in injury. The ghost of an old man has been seen standing at the foot of the stairs and unaccountable smells and sounds occur throughout the house.

Fobbing

Fisher's Farm dates back to 1470, but the barns were built at a later date. A gentleman is said to haunt the bedroom and visitors have unwittingly held a conversation with the unexpected guest. Sudden temperature drops from 16 to 13°C have been recorded. One owner of the farm placed a sword that he had found in Kent onto a timber beam in the living room area and one day it flew 8ft off the beam and almost hit someone!

The sound of someone opening and closing the front door of Peasant's Croft have been reported by people who have lived there. This sound is always followed by footsteps walking in the hallway, but investigation proved nobody to be there. The ancient Roman vineyard behind Peasant's Croft now resembles overgrown fields and a number of paranormal occurrences have been reported there: rattling chains have been heard and a white mist that resembles a human form has been seen moving up and down the hedgerow. People walking through the field have reported being pushed.

Great Waltham

Langley Manor was the site of a most tragic haunting that seems almost impossible to believe. Sir Charles Lee's daughter became frantic after being visited by the ghost of her deceased mother, who told her that she would die the next day. Doctors were summoned to calm the girl and, after being comforted by family, she was given a clean bill of health. Regardless of the doctor's diagnosis, she died the next day.

Aveley

Henry's Resteraunt used to be Kennington's House and is listed in the Domesday Book under the name 'Kelituna'. Staff have reported mysterious footsteps and a door in the main bar shakes as though someone is hammering on the other side as if trying to get in. Unexplained breezes gust through the building and objects are moved about.

two

HAUNTED CHURCHES

Bowers Gifford

If you take the B1464 from Sadlers Farm in Benfleet towards Pitsea town centre and drive through Bowers Gifford, you will come to a mini-roundabout at Gun Hill. Take the road to your left and it will take you to Basildon Crematorium, keep on driving and the road will take you steeply downhill along a narrow lane. The quaint St Margaret's Church sits at the end of this road, surrounded by old gravestones, snugly tucked in by a patchwork blanket of crop fields.

In the middle of the last century, parishioners that had stopped by to pray in silence were stunned as the organ began to be played by unseen hands. There have been no recent reports of a repeated musical performance, but you never feel alone when you stand among the ancient tombs.

St Margaret's Church, Bowers Gifford.
(Author's Collection)

Lane leading down to St Margaret's Church, Bowers Gifford. (Author's Collection)

Another strange phenomenon reported in that area were the electrical faults experienced by people driving down the lane to the church. Headlamps would flicker and die, plunging the road into pitch darkness, much to the terror of the car's occupants! Even more terrifyingly, people have also experienced brake failure!

Chelmsford

A local legend exists in Chelmsford that if you run around All Saints' Church thirteen times, the ghost of an angry nun appears to the challenger and chases after them! A more serious ghost tale is that of a man in top hat and cloak that has been seen striding down Patching Hall Lane near St John Payne Catholic School. He is said to have a pale, drawn complexion and has a fearful look etched on his face.

Basildon

In 1964 reports began coming into the local press and police station regarding sightings of a monk dressed in red robes. He was seen 'floating' across Church Road, off Clay Hill Road, and vanished into thin air in the churchyard of Holy Cross Church. People would see him as they went to work at the new Ford Tractor Plant in the mornings and tales of the Phantom Red Monk were becoming legendary.

Holy Cross Church, Basildon. (Author's Collection)

One man, incensed by this apparent ghost stopping him dead in his tracks in the mornings, decided to debunk the prankster by riding his bike directly at the Red Monk. The terrified man sailed right through the monk and claimed he was chilled to the bone as he passed through the phantom. Another person who did this, purely by accident, was a cleaner who was unfortunate enough to ride through the monk while on her way to work. She described the feeling as chilling and clammy.

Unfortunately, these people appear to have been victims of an elaborate hoax. In 2004 a group of locals came forward and claimed responsibility for the 'phantom monk', using a projector to show the image of a monk against the autumn fog. The group even left recordings of rattling chains in the church!

Church Road in Basildon is also said to be haunted by two other spectres: a young girl who was hit and killed by a horse-drawn cart and a mysterious and terrifying ghost that would grab people from behind and hurl them over nearby bushes! When the victim got to their feet, there was nobody in sight. Grown men would walk home in pairs from the nearby Bull public house (more recently The Powerhouse, but now residential flats have been built on the site) in fear of attack by this mischievous ghoul.

Fobbing

The fourteenth-century tower of St Michael's Church was used by British soldiers as a lookout to protect the coastline from invading Dutch and French forces. In later

St Michael's Church, Fobbing.
(Author's Collection)

years the tower was used by pirates and smugglers. Locals tell of a French Pirate who was buried in a grave against the walls of the churchyard and his grave would glow at night. The ghost of the pirate would be seen looking down at his own grave. This tale appears to be an urban legend, as many other coastal villages also lay claim to this story. The church also allegedly has a history of Black Magic. Strange unexplained smells have been reported and gravestones have been warm to touch one moment, then very cold the next.

Canewdon

Canewdon, a small sleepy village tucked inland below the River Crouch and a short distance from Wallasea Island, is known as the 'village of witches'. At one point, thirteen witches lived in the tiny village, and to this day the whole village is closed off on Halloween. On this day, all manner of outsiders try to access St Nicholas' Church to cast spells, dabble in black magic or to see if they can spot a ghost in the surrounding area. Any outsider wishing to pay Canewdon an uninvited visit on 31 October is met by a police roadblock and turned away. During a recent roadblock, officers noticed a figure cross the lane behind them and disappear into the bushes. Suspecting someone had crept behind the roadblock officers gave chase on foot, but no one was to be seen in the bushes, fields or lane; there was no other hiding place.

There are many legends that tell of a spell that can be cast if you walk around the church so many times, a certain way. One myth is that if you walk around the church clockwise three times at midnight the ghosts and witches will appear! There are other variations of this mythical spell: that the Devil will appear, or you will have an image of the future. Unfortunately, it is all pure folklore, but great tales all the same.

St Nicholas, Canewdon.
(Author's Collection)

In all seriousness, the village is said to be host to many spooks. The wife of one of the previous vicars reported seeing the ghost in the driveway of the rectory. Also at the church many people have seen a faceless woman who only appears on moonless nights. She drifts slowly through the western gate towards the River Crouch. The most famous Canewdon ghost has to be the witch who was buried at the crossroads in the centre of the village. She is said to rise up from the ground and walk to the River Crouch, where she has been seen walking across the water.

Despite a live television investigation in 2004 that followed the trail of Matthew Hopkins, he never actually visited Canewdon. However, two witches were arrested and tried in the village during the fourteenth century: Rose Pye in 1580 and Cicily Makyn in 1585 and rearrested as 'Mrs/Goodwife Makins' in 1590 (there were no spelling guidelines in those days). Rose Pye is the accused witch who allegedly haunts the crossroads. Despite common belief, there are no records of either of these women actually being executed. There is, however, a great possibility that one of the women was buried at the crossroads after a natural death. Maybe the villagers were still superstitious about the fact the women could have been witches and thought it best to bury them there in case they came back to haunt the village!

Many people have carried out investigations around the area of St Nicholas' Church. On one occasion a group of friends descended on Canewdon to carry out an investigation. Fully charged batteries in their torches and cameras were drained, strange shadows were seen and one member suffered pains during a séance, which forced the group to abandon the experiment. On another occasion strange lights were witnessed in the churchyard and unexplained noises were recorded, including one which sounded like someone chopping wood, not unusual you may think, but this was after 3 a.m! The sound then stopped after almost a minute before the sound of footsteps could be heard walking away from the group!

three

GHOSTS OF WAR

East Tilbury

Coalhouse Fort at East Tilbury was built in 1861-74, quite some time after neighbouring Tilbury Fort, which was built in the sixteenth century for Henry VIII. Roman remains, dating from AD 43 or shortly after, have been found in East Tilbury, and at some point during AD 600 St Cedd erected a church in the area.

The site saw action in both world wars before being bought by Thurrock Council in 1962. Loud sighs and the sounds of men playing a game of poker have been heard echoing through the building and tunnel systems. Many ghost hunts, séances and Ouija sessions have left interesting results, including the recording of electronic voice phenomena, cold spots noted by thermometers, the draining of batteries in torches and cameras, orbs and even misty apparitions. Sounds recorded include sighs, footsteps and a strange dragging noise.

Hadstock

The B1052 near Hadstock was the scene of a fascinating incident in November 1993. Exactly fifty years after an aircraft crashed during the Second World War, the ghost of the dead United States Army Air Force (USAAF) pilot appeared in the backseat of a lady's car as she drove by the crash site. The lady was completely unaware of the tragedy that had occurred half a century earlier.

Coalhouse Fort, East Tilbury. (Author's Collection)

Ridgewell

This tiny village and the surrounding area was taken over by the USAAF during the Second World War and was home to the 381st Bomb Group. During its stay, it carried out daylight air raids over France and Germany and flight squadrons took off daily at around 6.30 a.m. to reach their target destination.

Many years after the war had ended, people began to report ghostly lights across the disused airfield. People also heard men shouting and the distinct revving of Jeep engines and, most amazingly of all, the sound of screeching tyres on tarmac as if a plane was landing. Very occasionally people reported hearing the sound of crashing, just like the sound of badly damaged bombers landing without their undercarriage down. Ghostly airmen are still reported to roam the area.

Hornchurch

Hornchurch Country Park is said to be the site of much paranormal activity connected with an airfield that ran across the site, RAF Hornchurch. This airfield was built here on the site of Suttons Farm, specifically to protect London from Zeppelin attack during the First World War. Park walkers and staff from the nearby hospital have reported seeing the ghosts of men dressed in RAF uniforms and people have heard the faint

Ashingdon Hill. (Author's Collection)

sound of propeller engine aircraft. Could the fact that many features of the original airbase such as pillboxes and gun placements remain be the reason that so many ghosts still stay?

Ashingdon

This peaceful village was once host to one of the bloodiest battles in British history, the Battle of Ashingdon, fought between the Anglo-Saxons and the invading Danish army. The fact that grass would not grow back at the hill where the battle commenced was considered paranormal for many years. Grass now grows there, but the haunting sounds of clashing swords and battle cries are still reported until this day, mainly around the area of the church of St Andrew's Minster.

four

GHOSTLY APPARITIONS AND STRANGE OCCURRENCES

Mersea Island

Mersea Island, England's most easterly inhabited island, has an array of ghostly visitors. West Mersea is most populated and has several caravan holiday parks. As you travel across to East Mersea, houses become few and far between and you find yourself alone, gazing out across fields towards the North Sea.

To access the island you must wait until low tide to cross a causeway, aptly named 'the Strood', which was constructed by the Romans in AD 700. This is the site where two sailors, driving toward the Peldon Rose Inn, hit a man dressed as a Roman centurion, who suddenly appeared in front of their car late one night in 1970. There was no bump or bang and when they got up to investigate they saw the wispy figure of a man floating off down the road!

Legend also speaks of two tragic Viking brothers whose wraiths are still locked in a fierce battle over the love of the same woman. Their ghosts still fight on Ray Island. People have also reported hearing the sounds of heavy marching and men fighting with swords.

Another of Mersea Island's ghosts is a ghostly dog. The men who deliver goods into the cellars of the White Hart Inn are always complaining about the pesky dog that gets under their feet when they are carrying in crates. However, the landlords have always insisted that there is no dog at the inn and further inspection of the cellars always proves the point!

The Strood, Mersea Island. (Author's Collection)

On the north side of East Mersea churchyard lies the caged grave of 15-year-old Sarah Wrench. Not only was this girl buried on the cold unlit side of the churchyard, but her grave has a cage over it. What terrible deeds must Sarah have been accused of to have been laid to rest in such a way? Despite reports of Sarah being laid north to south, this is untrue, and as the photographs show, her grave is laid east to west like the others. Rumours about Sarah's character range from her being a witch to being possessed by demons.

Hullbridge

Early one evening in October 1970 a yachtsman and his passenger were driving around Brandy Hole when his car broke down. The driver got out, lifted the bonnet of the vehicle and started to look for signs of what could have happened. After a few minutes of checking the engine and radiator, the yachtsman noticed a figure was standing next to the car, watching silently. At first he was not alarmed as he assumed the man was his passenger, but as he focused on him he realised that the man, a fisherman, was invisible from the waist down! At that moment the man dematerialized and the shocked yachtsman ran to see where the fisherman had gone. His passenger stepped out of the car as he saw his friend was clearly distressed, but the passenger had not seen a thing.

Sarah Wrench's grave can be seen tucked in at the north-west corner of East Mersea Church. (Author's Collection)

The inscription on the iron plaque on Sarah Wrench's grave, East Mersea. (Author's Collection)

St Osyth

St Osyth's Priory is a magnificent building, dating mostly from around the twelfth century and is claimed to be the oldest monastic foundation surviving in Essex. St Osyth herself was an Anglo-Saxon princess in the seventh century who was forcibly married to King Sighere, King of the East Saxons. Osyth took her chance to flee the wedding when Sighere was tempted away from the feast to hunt a white stag that was spotted nearby. Tearfully, she fled to the safety of local East Anglican bishops. King Sighere was devastated that the bishops had accepted her vow of chastity, but they persuaded him to allow Osyth some land to build a convent. Osyth was presented the village of Chich.

In AD 700, Danish pirates came ashore and took the land. Osyth was beheaded in Nun's Wood after she refused to renounce her Christian faith. The Danish executioners were horrified when water gushed from her head (creating the stream that still runs through Nun's Wood). She then stood up, picked up her head and walked to the village church, holding the head up at arms length. She banged on the church door several times before slumping to the ground. The church canonised St Osyth after hearing the story of her devout faith and Chich was renamed St Osyth. It is said that on 7 October each year, St Osyth repeats her headless walk and is seen in the churchyard holding her severed head.

Brentwood

The White Hart, also in the High Street, harbours a mischievous ghost that taps people on the shoulder and moves objects around. Mild poltergeist activity has been reported and another property in Brentwood High Street, No. 133, is said to be a place of terrifying occurrences. Ghostly laughter echoes down corridors and across rooms, severe drops and increases in temperature are reported, plus animals are said to react violently upon entering the building. The Fountain Head in Ingrave Road is also host to poltergeist activity: exploding bottles and moving furniture are the main occurrences that have been reported.

Linford

Walton Hall Museum has had reports of a ghostly figure that walks the fields behind the hall and suddenly vanishes into thin air. Could this be the same figure that haunts the main barn? This shade is seen to walk across the room, stopping outside the ladies' toilets before stabbing a knife into a nearby pillar and then walking off. Witnesses describe him as a short man with a 'weathered face'. During one investigation, three people witnessed a dark shadowy figure appear in a doorway near the kitchen area. The figure moved slowly towards the exit. This repeated again thirty seconds later. The figure was estimated to be about 5ft 6in in height. Footsteps were also heard.

Chelmsford

Springfield Place used to be haunted by a mischievous ghost that would harass all who passed by. It was said to terrorise anyone in the area around the churchyard.

The white building that houses the BBC Essex studios is said to have not just one ghost clattering around in its attic, but at least five! Investigations and independent witnesses have all reported an old lady; a girl aged about 9; a girl in her late teens; an angry man, and a boy in his mid-teens. The 9-year-old girl is said to be a happy little soul, but craves attention. Perhaps most interesting of all is the description of the girl in her late teens; she is allegedly called Amy and killed herself by jumping from one of the windows. She had been raped and had become pregnant; the angry man who haunts the house is said to be her attacker. The young boy has also been identified as being a 15-year-old called Tom.

Tilbury

While firemen were still stationed at the Old Fire Station in Tilbury town they reported seeing the ghost of a lady. She was thought to be a woman who had collapsed while walking past the station and was brought inside to rest in bed, and then subsequently died.

In the 1960s a fire officer, wracked with guilt after the death of two crewmen on his shout, hanged himself from the attic hatch. Local residents tell of how the old night-watchman would walk around the building with his dog. Firemen have reported hearing a very loud 'growl' while walking along the fire station's corridors.

Possibly the strangest story of all is that of a fireman who was carrying a tray of tea for his colleagues in the activity room. He noticed someone walking toward him so he stepped to one side, but as they got nearer he realised the figure was a ghost! As he looked down at the tray, the tea cups had vanished. When he returned to the kitchen, all the cups were washed and drying out on the drainer. Firemen visiting from neighbouring stations tell of how they refuse to go back to the old Tilbury fire station and the men are definitely happier at their new home.

Upminster

The clubhouse at Upminster Golf Club previously housed a monastery over 800 years ago. People have reported seeing the ghost of a young girl in a white dress in the first-floor corridor of the clubhouse. She is also said to be the same ghost that haunts the flat belonging to the club's secretary. There is a legend that the girl was kidnapped in the 1600s, hidden in the old monastery, which was then a manor house, and eventually murdered. Her body was entombed in the walls of a room that overlooks the car park.

Shoreline, Walton on the Naze. (Author's Collection)

Ingatestone

Ingatestone railway station has an invisible phantom whose heavy footsteps have been heard crossing over the footbridge and walking past bewildered passengers awaiting the next train.

Walton on the Naze

The original church for this cosy seaside town was washed into the sea by the ever-rising tide levels in 1798. Whenever a bad storm is approaching people have reported hearing 'ghostly' bells tolling beneath the waves. The church eerily reappeared one afternoon in January 1928 during a rare low tide caused by a violent storm, its brickwork caked in seaweed and barnacles. Soft, shifting sands prevented the curious townspeople from walking out to the church and within a few short hours the tide crept back in and the church was reclaimed by the North Sea.

Many years later, a local walking his dog noticed that the tide had receded quite far back and through low cloud could see mysterious figures about 300 yards from the shore bending down as if to pick things up before moving away toward the cliff area. All this time the man's dog, which was usually eager to pull forward, was pulling back and seemed disturbed. The man told a friend what he had witnessed and the pair agreed to meet up and walk their dogs in that area the following day at the same time. Sure enough, about 200-300 yards offshore was a group of mysterious figures, all carrying something. They all walked away into the distance before vanishing into low cloud. It was believed that this could have been the ghosts of the villagers buried at Walton on the Naze's old churchyard and they were returning to find their own remains. I have come across a very similar, and far more famous, story for the town of Dunwich.

A ghostly fisherman has been seen on Walton's Pier and modern-day anglers have allegedly held a conversation with this stranger, who is dressed in soft leather waders and unusual attire. The local fisherman have returned to check their lines and then turned to see that the mysterious man has vanished along with all his rods, nets and other equipment. It would have been impossible for the fisherman to have gathered his gear and walked, or even run, the length of the open pier in the time it takes for the other anglers to glance away before looking back.

Basildon

Workers at Basildon Hospital in the 1980s would tell of how lights would come on in ward twelve, near reception, even though it was unused and padlocked shut with heavy chains! They repeatedly had to call out caretakers and security to unlock the ward so the lights could be switched off and the rooms searched for possible intruders.

One worker spoke of an incident that occurred over in the M.I. Unit one evening. Coughing could be heard emanating from the men's toilets, which sounded quite violent. All the staff on duty commented on the awful sound until it became so bad that they couldn't stand by any longer without checking that the unfortunate gentleman was okay. The lady who told me about this event explained how she knocked on the door of the men's toilets and called out to the man inside to see if he was okay. She could hear running water, but the coughing had stopped and there was no reply. Worried about the gentleman's welfare, she entered the toilets and all was silent; no running water, no coughing and more chillingly, no person in sight! The stalls were empty and the windows were locked!

Braintree

A phantom cyclist that charges into traffic, causing mayhem in a road near Faulkbourne Hall, has terrified drivers and fellow cyclists for many years.

Canewdon

In the 1960s some villagers in Canewdon reported seeing the ghost of a man dressed in the attire of a crusader in Larkhill Road, but one wonders if this was just a drunken fool on his way home from a fancy dress party!

Chingford

Chingford Mount Cemetery was built on land previously owned by Lady Hamilton, lover of Lord Nelson, and is reputedly haunted by a phantom horse rider. Unexplained footsteps can be heard on the pathway outside Cemetery Lodge, accompanied by disembodied voices and a spine-tingling whining. It has been said that the phantom rider is none other than Dick Turpin, riding his horse, Black Bess. Another theory is that it is Lord Nelson himself, but it is more likely to be a lost member of a royal hunting party that tore across the Hamilton Estate long ago.

Foulness Island

This huge but sparsely populated island is only accessible via a ferry from Burnham-on-Crouch or by road from Great Wakering and has a history that dates back to Roman times, as archaeological digs have proven. The island is owned by the Government and is largely inaccessible to the general public because the southern part of the island is mainly used for testing shells, explosives, bullets and other dangerous weapons. This has been the case since the Second World War, although it has been less top secret in recent years and the houses and farms in Churchend and Courtsend have remained the same for decades. The island also has a history of smuggling and piracy around its North Sea shores. This is mainly due to the dozens of waterways that cross the island, and the shores remain largely empty of passers-by who could have stumbled across these criminals.

Many years ago, before a large section of the island was reclaimed from the sea for farmland, a ship had sunk just off shore. Years later, some islanders still say that at times you can see the ghostly vessel sailing across the fields!

A place on the island nicknamed 'Lucky Corner' is the haunting site of a woman who allegedly carries her head under her arm! Not such a lucky corner for the unfortunate lady! Also in Foulness is a maid who haunts a pond where she had drowned herself after becoming pregnant by her master, before he threw the poor girl out. She is said to circle the pond and has even accompanied shocked passers-by. Many servicemen and islanders have told of having spooky feelings about certain areas and experiencing the spine-tingling feeling of being watched.

Southend-on-Sea

The world's longest pleasure pier at Southend-on-Sea has a colourful history. At the beginning of the Second World War, the Dunkirk evacuations were organised on the pier. Numerous vessels have also struck the mile and three quarter deck and it suffered two catastrophic fires in the late-twentieth century.

In 2004 an enterprise called 'SSHAPE' began work to revamp the Victorian entrance and make a feature of the architecture so that the seafront could be dragged into

The creek between Foulness Island and Havengore Island. (Author's Collection)

The new lift construction at Southend-on-Sea seafront. (Author's Collection)

The outline of the old Victorian steps can be seen clearly against one of the pier's cafes, Southend-on-Sea. (Author's Collection)

the twenty-first century. By the summer, the pier entrance had already had a grand unveiling and works on the new cliff lift and staircases had begun. In order to fit this new structure in, the cliff face had to be excavated and the old stone staircase, which comprised of two whitewashed concrete flights of stairs that hugged against the west side of the arches under the pier, had to be removed.

As work progressed, workers began reporting an odd black shadow that would appear where the old staircase used to be. This turned into reports of a full-blown apparition of a woman dressed in black, who floated in mid air, as if still standing on the stairs. In early September, a constable from Southend Police reported a disturbance at the site and that a couple of workers had literally run off in terror. Apparently, one of the workers had been engrossed in some work by the old stairs when he clearly heard a female say in his ear, 'You shouldn't be doing this!' He turned, saw the woman in black and fled. Upon speaking to nearby shop owners, they were not surprised to hear about the phantom woman and went on to tell me stories of how late-night revellers would stumble across the ghostly apparition on the stairs on a regular basis.

In August 1923, the captain of a ship cruising down the Thames Estuary off shore at Southend-on-Sea, was on deck with one of his crew when they spotted a creature rise up out of the water beside their vessel. It raised its snake-like neck twice out of the water, about 2 meters high before vanishing.

Canvey Island

This densely populated island is just 5 miles from east to west and 3 miles north to south and has only been inhabited since the 1600s when Dutchman Cornelius Vermyden and his colleagues made the marshland habitable. Could he be the ghostly lone Dutchman seen wandering the northern parts of the island carrying a sack? Although only inhabited since the 1600s, the land was used as grazing pasture right back to Roman times.

Canvey Island's lake has its own 'Lady of the Lake' in the form of a woman who was drowned there many years ago. Local stories are sketchy and some even say it was a man who drowned, but the majority speak of a female ghost who has wandered the area since her horse-drawn carriage plummeted into the lake. A recent clean up of the lake found the remains of two horses and fragments of a wooden carriage.

The story of the 'The Black Man' and 'The White Lady' is believed to be a mythical tale conjured up by smugglers to stop people wandering onto the 'saltings' and finding their smuggled goods. It was said that the 'Black Man' offered a price for your soul, while the 'White Woman' tempted you to dance with her. Men often spoke of trying to chase away the figures, only to watch them vanish before their eyes!

Many night fishermen have reported seeing a tall, burly Viking standing on mudflats at The Point, on the far eastern side of the island. It is believed that he was left behind by his fleet and waited for his ship to return; only to drown in the rising tide.

A farm hand at the now long-demolished Knightswick Farm watched a nun approach the farm from the fields one afternoon from the porch of the farmhouse.

Canvey Island, as seen from Hadleigh Castle, with Kent in far distance. (Author's Collection)

The Lake, Canvey Island. (Author's Collection)

Puzzled as to why the nun had walked across the muddy fields, the girl left the porch and walked toward the nun as she intended to greet her. Suddenly, the nun began to vanish into the ground as she walked!

Bradwell-on-Sea

The tiny Catholic church of St Peter's on the Wall, near Bradwell-on-Sea, is one of Britain's oldest churches and was almost used as target practice during the Second World War by the Royal Navy thinking it was just a barn, but escaped destruction thanks to a quick-thinking map reader! Strange shadows and mists have been seen in the vicinity of the church and many people have reported hearing the sound of horse's hooves approaching, although there was clearly no a horse in sight.

In 1967 the ghost of a Roman soldier was seen here, riding a horse where the ancient Roman Fort called Othona stood, built to protect the land from invading Norseman. The road from Othona to Danbury, Colchester and Chelmsford is still in use today and connects the ancient site to the village of Bradwell-on-Sea. People have heard horses' hooves and marching soldiers along this stretch of road. However, these stories of ghostly horses and Romans could have been cooked up by smugglers that used the crumbling fort and the Chapel of St Peter's between 1700 and 1850. The story would scare visiting Revenue men away and keep the smugglers from being found out.

Coggeshall

This sleepy village in mid-Essex is said not only to be situated on a ley line, but crossed by two of them. Ley lines are said to be powerful beams of energy, which are connected to the Earth's magnetic field. Coggershall is also acclaimed as 'the most haunted village in East Anglia'. A number of creepy historical facts litter Coggeshall's ancient history and make the ghost stories in the village a little easier to comprehend.

St Peter's Road used to be known as Dead Lane, and East Street was known as Gallows Street. There were also a set of gallows for public executions, on the site of the former village of Tollgate. A number of buildings in the village have seen discoveries of domestic cats buried in walls, shocking the builders renovating the properties. It is also widely rumoured that the warrior queen, Boudicea, is buried in the village with her chariot and jewels.

Coggeshall's best-loved ghost is the ghost of Robin the Woodcutter. He was a local tradesman who worked in the woods on the land of Coggeshall Abbey and once carved a beautiful statue called, 'The Angel of the Christmas Mysteries', which was unfortunately lost after being hidden during the Reformation. The sound of his ghostly axe, accompanied by cheerful whistling, is often heard emanating from the woods. Robin himself has been seen wandering near the brook, known locally as Robin's Brook, since the 1600s.

Chapel in the grounds of Coggeshall Abbey. (Author's Collection)

Little Baddow

In November 2001, a young couple moored their 24ft houseboat near Grace's Walk on the River Chelmer in Little Baddow. While settling down for the night, they heard footsteps on the roof, a sound like gravel being thrown, and lights flashing around the boat. When the owner went to investigate, expecting teenagers to be the culprits, he jumped out to catch whoever was walking about on the deck, but was surprised to find there was no one there. He looked on the towpath, but saw no one and noticed that there was no gravel or stones on the nearby footpath. In terror, they decided to steer the narrowboat away from the area and the following morning reported the incident to the proprietor of Blackwater Boats.

The owner of a local boat company told the couple about the legend of Grace's Ghost. Grace was a young woman who committed suicide in a pond near Grace's Walk sometime in the 1700s or 1800s after her uncle relentlessly abused her. Her tortured wraith has been spotted numerous times riding on a horse on the bridge or towpath. Now several of the places where Grace has been spotted in Little Baddow have been named after her, including: Grace's Lane, Grace's Walk, Great Grace's Farm and Great Graces.

Grace's Lane. (Author's Collection)

Great Baddow

At St Mary's Church in Great Baddow people have often reported seeing soldiers dressed in Civil War attire, standing outside the church watching the building. Inside, people have seen a monk floating down the aisle, exiting the door on the west side of the church. Locals believe that he is connected with the mysterious secret tunnels that were discovered underneath the church.

Molram's Lane is haunted by the friendly ghost from whom the lane took its name. Molly Ram was a local landowner who loved her home so much, it seems she was reluctant to leave. Molly was known to be fond of a drop of ale and was often seen in her local in nearby Sandon. One day her husband returned from work to find that the house was empty and no housework had been done, and there was no food! He stormed down to the pub to find Molly propping up the bar and a little worse for wear. He dragged her out by her hair. Her body was found in a ditch in the lane and little is known of what occurred, but no record can be found of her husband being arrested. People walking down Molrams Lane late at night have spoken of an 'evil presence' that follows you and you can almost feel someone's breath on your collar!

In a private cottage on a hill near Jay's Green, the owners are said to hear footsteps most nights at 9 p.m. The footsteps are heard all over the cottage and no cause can be found for them.

Maldon

There have been sightings of a White Lady at the old Maldon railway station since the line was in use from 1958. One station master saw the apparition numerous times up until 1975, eleven years before the track was demolished. The temperature on platform 2 would drop dramatically, denoting her presence, terrifying any late-night passengers that waited for the last train to Chelmsford. The station master was so petrified by the wailing coming from the darkened platform and the other odd sounds that he slept with a shotgun under his pillow for many years!

The line was later closed and the station left to fall into disrepair. Then, in the 1980s, a builder snapped it up to renovate the building and transform it into a public house. It was during these renovations that the builders made a bizarre and chilling discovery beneath the station floorboards: a damp patch in the soil resembling an adult-sized body shape. The builders dug up the soil and left it, only to find the shape had re-appeared. Since the pub opened, both staff and customers have complained of ice-cold drops in temperature and seen a 'white misty form' near the washrooms. Some terrified members of staff have even quit their jobs! Her identification remains a complete mystery. The site is now used as offices.

The old Maldon Railway Station building. (Author's Collection)

Prittlewell Priory. (Author's Collection)

Prittlewell

Although Prittlewell is regarded generally as part of Southend-on-Sea, it is a village in its own right, with an ancient history that far precedes that of Southend-on-Sea. Priory Park is a beautiful park that is calm and serene, away from the bustling seaside town of Southend-on-Sea. Prittle Brook is a stream that babbles and trickles from the River Roach, through Priory Park. The brook is accompanied by a public footpath and dips under hundreds of streets through Prittlewell, Westcliff and Leigh.

The park gates are locked at night, but if you are walking through the park at dusk, you may witness the ghost of a monk who haunts the area around the museum. Locals swear that he is responsible for suddenly sending the ducks on the pond into a frenzy. An archaeological dig in the 1960s discovered the grave of a monk, buried in such a way that showed he was a 'disgraced monk'. This may explain why his spirit still roams the vicinity of the priory. The museum used to be the Priory of the Blessed Virgin Mary and the stone of Rainaldus is displayed inside.

Further archaeological digs in the early part of the twenty-first century revealed the burial place of the 'Saxon King of Prittlewell', whose remains were excavated and are now preserved in a local museum.

Prittlewell Priory. (Author's Collection)

The pond, Priory Park, Prittlewell. (Author's Collection)

five

PUBLIC HOUSES, INNS AND HOTELS

Thorpe-le-Soken

The Bell Inn is reputedly haunted by the ghost of Kitty Canham. She was a beautiful young woman who once lived in the cottage adjoining the inn. She married the local vicar, but then mysteriously vanished without trace. She returned to Thorpe-le-Soken many years later with another husband. Neither man had any idea that they were both married to the same woman, but as she was dying they made their peace and tended her until she passed away, burying her as she had wished in the parish churchyard.

Kitty is said to have never left Thorpe-le-Soken after dying and is thought to be the ghostly female figure seen in one of the guest rooms of the Bell Inn. People have reported feeling an odd presence while there and in 1972 a huge heavy wardrobe in the room moved during the night. On another occassion, he sheets on the spare bed were messed up as though someone had slept in it!

Tragedy struck during the late 1990s when fire tore through the ancient inn and destroyed a large section of it. Despite this, the large painting of Kitty that hangs in the bar area remained untouched. The inn has now been restored to its former glory.

Mucking

The old village pub was called the Crown Inn and, in the mid-1800s, a young man staying there became ill with cholera and died. The bed he died on was taken outside but the village children began playing on it and a few of the children died that very day! The disembodied voices of children playing are still heard throughout the village, even though the school closed long ago and even the school bell is still sometimes heard ringing.

The Bell Inn and Kitty's cottage, Thorpe-le-Soken. (Author's Collection)

The Thorn Inn, Mistley. (Author's Collection)

Mistley

Shadowy figures have been seen beside the Robert Adam Swan Fountain, around Mistley Towers and at the infamous 'Hopping Bridge', where it is rumoured that Hopkins met his death.

The Thorn Hotel in Mistley is one of the places where Hopkins used to 'interrogate' his victims. His ghost has been seen during the daytime in one of the hotel's upstairs rooms and is described as being eerily life-like. A mysterious hooded figure and a Grey Lady have also been seen throughout the hotel; one wonders which of his victims these strange shades are. With the pure horror that went on in these three villages during the Essex witch trials of the 1600s, it is hardly surprising to learn that their tortured wraiths still lurk in the shadows.

Great Oakley

The Maybush Inn was haunted by a petite Oriental lady wearing a kimono, who floated through walls on the first floor of the inn. The sound of objects crashing to the ground, usually followed by hurried footsteps, and most unusually the sound of rolling marbles, were common occurrences. One 1970s landlord, who had previously laughed off the alleged hauntings, was shocked to see the Oriental woman floating across his bedroom, disappearing into the walls and reappearing with an object before vanishing. Activity has reportedly ceased now.

Ingatestone

The Star Inn in the village of Ingatestone is haunted by a pet dog that died there in 1914. Many people have spotted him over the last thirty years, describing a small, black, spotted dog wandering around.

Benfleet

Benfleet Conservative Club is a popular watering hole, close to St Mary's Church and the old Benfleet pubs, is said to harbour the ghost of Lord Horatio Nelson's lover, Lady Hamilton. Many members will tell you of tales of how Lady Hamilton has been seen wandering the corridors of the sixteenth-century building, looking for her lover. Lady Hamilton died, aged 50, in 1815 and had used the building to secretly rendezvous with Nelson when he returned from the Napoleonic conflicts. Contractors working on the building have felt someone watching over them as they work, dogs have run from empty rooms whimpering, and shadows, cracks and bangs have been seen and heard by many.

Purfleet

The Royal Hotel's Room 31 is reputedly haunted by the ghosts of a young couple. The young girl was murdered by her boyfriend after an argument about his gambling habit. The room remains the least used at the hotel, as people won't sleep there. Staff have also seen figures standing at the far end of the balcony area of the upper restaurant and also walking through the kitchen. Items have been moved and, late one night in the Longridge Bar, some drinks flew off a table and smashed onto the floor.

Sible Hedingham

The White Horse public house in Sible Hedingham is home to an invisible entity that taps customers on the shoulder. Staff and customers have been alarmed when they feel it running past them in the pub's corridors.

The 300-year-old Bell Inn in St James Street is said to be haunted by two ghosts: one is a mysterious monk who died in a fire at the Bell Inn and the other is a young girl with black hair.

Great Leighs

St Anne's Castle claims to be the oldest inn in England and stands on the Main Road which runs parallel to the A131 Great Leighs Bypass. In 1170 Thomas Becket was murdered in Canterbury and pilgrims on there way to pay there respects would stop at St Anne's Castle Inn to eat and rest for the night. The swinging pub sign has an archbishop's mitre painted on it with Thomas Becket's date of birth.

Maldon

The King's Head in the High Street, Maldon, dates back long before 1532 and has been host to a poltergeist that was first recorded in 1946. Rumour says that extensions built during the seventeenth, eighteenth and nineteenth centuries were built over plague burial sites. During one time when the floor was taken up, dozens of human bones were discovered, but it is also believed that one of the previous landlords could have been a serial killer, preying on wealthy travellers. Footsteps have been heard running up and down the stairs and across the hall in the dead of night and people have been trapped in the upstairs lavatory, despite the door being easy to open and close at all other times! Objects have moved from room to room with no explanation and placed in doorways.

St Anne's Castle, Great Leighs. (Author's Collection)

Stock

The Bear Inn has stood in the village square at Stock for over 400 years. In the late 1800s the pub's ostler, Charlie Wilson, earned himself the nickname 'Spider' due to his strange sideways walk. Spider's drunken 'party trick' was to disappear up the tap-room chimney and re-emerge from the fireplace in the bar. One Christmas Eve, Spider got into the chimney, but didn't reappear in the bar. Pub goers tried to coax Spider down, but he chose to ignore them and sat in the bacon curing loft at the junction of the chimneys. Tired of his antics, they lit a small fire in the grate to smoke him out, but it is thought he suffocated and died. Allegedly, his 'well-cured' remains still sit in the chimney to this day!

Spider's ghost has been seen exiting the chimney at night. Witnesses describe him to be wearing white breeches and leather boots. He never gets up to mischief, instead choosing to contentedly flit freely around this timeless establishment.

Brentwood

The Swan public house, High Street, Brentwood, was previously named the Argent and the Gunn before receiving the name the Swan in 1783. It has recently been renamed Sugar Hut Village and modernised. The inn is haunted by the ghost of 19-year-old

The Swan, Brentwood. (Author's Collection)

William Hunter who was held there for two days in March 1555, before being burned at the stake for his Protestant beliefs.

William claimed that he had seen a vision of his death in a dream and went on to explain the events before being taken to The Butts on Shenfield Common. Since then, doors have been locked and unlocked by unseen hands, taps have been turned on and off and objects have been moved around the building. Any dog entering the bar is left whimpering in anguish. In 1963 the landlord's daughter saw the figure of a man with a hat follow her mother across the landing. Six years later another landlord's daughter refused to sleep in the pub after a terrifying night being subjected to all sorts of paranormal activity.

In the inn, copper name plates have been hurled across rooms, lights have been clicked on and off and objects have vanished and reappeared in other parts of the inn. Another time, a telephone in a locked room became unhinged from its mountings and was hurled across the room! Staff have repeatedly heard loud bangs emanating from the cellars, and furniture has moved around during the night.

Room 14 at the New World Inn in Great Warley Street is the haunting place of a previous landlady Mrs de Rougemont. The pub is allegedly so haunted that it is 'impossible to spend the night there'. The sounds of a party in full swing are some of the many noises that echo through the night at the New World Inn.

Saffron Walden

The Sun Inn on the corner of Market Hill and Church Street was host to Oliver Cromwell during the Civil War. It is now no longer a public house and inn, but split into various different businesses. A noisy poltergeist that moves furniture and makes loud bangs and crashes has often made people believe that the building is being ransacked by burglars. Could the mysterious shade of a Cromwellian soldier be responsible for this bizarre activity?

The Cross Keys on the corner of King Street and High Street also has Civil War ties and a ghostly figure is said to run down a dead-end passage every Christmas Eve before vanishing into thin air.

Coggeshall

The White Hart Hotel in Coggeshall is haunted by a mysterious figure that wanders the older parts of the building. It is mostly reported in the Guest's Lounge, which is the oldest part of the entire establishment. Cradle House, near the Old Rectory, is yet another haunted building, frequented by phantom monks that have been reported throughout the building and even dancing in the garden! In 1966 paranormal activity at 42 Church Street was reported: doors opening and closing, inexplicable smells and a strange mist that haunts the staircase.

Colchester

The Red Lion public house across the High Street from the Town Hall dates back to 1465 and is home to the ghost of Alice Miller, who was murdered here in 1633. She haunts rooms 5 and 6 of this Grade 1 listed building, and walks through a wall where a doorway once was. The doorway was bricked up over two centuries ago. She is also seen on the stairs and in the kitchen. Staff were warned never to mention the ghost for fear that it would put customers off going there; in fact the mere mention of the ghost could cost staff members their job! A member of staff slept over in the hotel one night and was woken at 3 a.m. by a sharp jolt, as though he had been given an electric shock. He jumped up and looked over towards the rocking chair next to his bed. The moonlight coming through the window had lit the chair, and it slowly began to rock back and forth and a woman materialised. She asked the man if he was all right and promptly vanished when he replied.

A solicitors' business in Head Lane used to be the King's Head Hotel and is situated where the 'Headgate' or main entrance to Colchester used to be. The building is haunted by a ghostly solider whose hobnail boots are heard stomping and clanking across the floor. Many say they have actually seen him walking in the doorway and say he is a Civil War solider, but whether he is a Parliamentarian or a Royalist remains

The White Hart, Coggeshall. (Author's Collection)

Braintree

The Angel in Notley Road is host to a spook that enjoys terrorising any dog that enters the pub. A shadowy figure and purposeful footsteps have been reported since the 1960s.

Old Lodge in Whethersford Road has been the scene of numerous sightings of a phantom policeman. Some report him in Victorian costume, others in more modern attire, but poltergeist activity in the vicinity of the sightings has put fear into the bravest visitor!

Chingford

The Royal Forest Hotel is haunted by a girl called Mary who died in a fire in the hotel in 1912. She is said to put fear into any animal that sets foot in the building and sits on the beds throughout the hotel. Many guests have reported feeling someone sit down at the end of the bed in the middle of the night.

to be discovered. One thing for certain is that the building used to house the offices of the Royalist commander, Sir Charles Lucas, even though Colchester itself was a staunchly Parliamentarian town.

The building that houses a bar near Scheregate Steps was built in the sixteenth century and is haunted by a female that walks the first floor. The peculiar thing about this haunting is that the woman's legs are in the floor from her knees down, but the people downstairs have never reported disembodied legs floating around the ceiling area!

The Fox and Fiddler pub is haunted by a young chambermaid called Sarah. This girl died in the early 1600s and is described as a cheeky ghost who loves to play pranks on customers and staff. The pub's cellars are connected to a large network of tunnels that run under the town. It is widely known that local highwaymen drank in The Fox and Fiddler, but the most prolific customer was in fact Matthew Hopkins, the Witchfinder General. He is rumoured to have been responsible for the death of Sarah and legend tells how he dragged her by her hair down to the cellar. She kicked and screamed relentlessly and was allegedly bricked up alive in one of the tunnel walls! If Matthew Hopkins truly did carry out this heinous act, he must have carried it out illegally, as I can find no trace of this girl being tried as a witch. Her shade has been seen by many members of staff, who describe her as blonde, wearing a chambermaid's outfit of a white lacy hat, and a white pinafore over a black dress. She will not allow objects to be moved in the attic, as this used to be her living space.

Sarah is usually quite well behaved these days, but if she takes a dislike to someone, she makes her feelings known. When a guest landlord stepped in to look after the pub when its owners went away on holiday, Sarah began distracting bar staff by touching them, making them jump in fright. She began to make sounds in the bottom bar while staff were wiping up glasses and when they would turn to investigate the noise, she would knock the glasses off the bar, smashing them on the floor!

A more humorous tale from Colchester is from a Chinese restaurant in the Vineyard Street area. A rather cheeky ghost called 'His Nibs' likes to appear while they are sitting in the toilet cubicles!

Dedham

The Sun Inn in Dedham's bustling High Street was once the workplace of a girl called Elsa. She was, as the tale goes, the last woman executed in Essex under the Witchcraft Act and her tortured wraith is said to wail throughout the building and its network of corridors. Legend has it that this is only heard just before a disaster happens. I cannot find any trace of this girl in the witch trial evidence, but she may have just been accused by locals of witchcraft and possibly killed illegally.

The Sun Inn, Dedham. (Author's Collection)

Earls Colne

Opposite Earls Colne Priory stands the Carved Angel public house, previously known as the Coachman's Inn. This pub has been the sight of a more recent and rare haunting in the form of a recently deceased young man. Most ghost sightings are obvious because of the way in which the apparition is dressed, but ghosts that wear jeans and trainers are harder to come by, as witnesses probably don't think to look twice.

A couple took over running the pub in the late 1990s and after settling in, invited one of their children to stay for a holiday along with their partner and 2-year-old son. The family soon became aware that whenever the child was alone in his bedroom he would babble away to an invisible person; this didn't strike anyone as particularly alarming as toddlers often chat away to themselves.

However, one day the child's grandmother was aware that the child was again chatting away in his room and crept in to see him staring into the corner, holding a one-way conversation. When she asked the child who he was speaking to, he simply said, 'That man! Who is he?' but the lady could see no one. She asked her grandson if he had seen this man before and the child said he was always there and played with him. After a week or so, the young family left to return home and the incident was forgotten until one bright sunny morning when the landlady awoke.

The pub owners had been decorating the rooms to their taste and had switched bedrooms to the room their grandson had slept in during his stay. The landlady got out of bed and opened the curtains to let in the sunlight and when she turned around there was a young man standing near the door of her bedroom. He was dressed in jeans and trainers, aged about 20 years old and smiled at her before vanishing into thin air! Startled by what she had just witnessed she woke her husband and he reminded her of what their grandson had said to her.

Some time later a young couple came into the bar and introduced themselves to the landlord; the young man's parents were the previous owners of the Coachman's Inn and he had grown up there. The landlord asked the young man if he was aware of any ghosts in the pub and described what his wife had seen. The young man became pale and told the landlord that the ghost was the reason that his parents had moved out of the pub. The ghost was that of his brother who was killed in a motorcycle accident and shortly after his death his ghost would appear in his old bedroom and on the staircase. The parents just found the haunting heartbreaking and were forced to leave their home to rebuild their lives.

Great Waltham

The Great Waltham public house was previously known as the Rose and Crown. When contractors began work on renovating the pub in 1980, they were plagued by unexplained knocks, bangs and crashes, but all ceased on the day of completion!

Tilbury

The World's End public house, tucked in snugly on the west side of Tilbury Fort's moat, used to be the haunt of highwayman Nick Nevison, known by his alias 'Swift Nick'. It is highly likely that the local term of 'to nick' actually originated from his name! He is the most likely suspect for the ghost that has been seen leaning over a child's bed in one of the upstairs rooms and reigniting fires that had been quelled or burned out, sometimes for days!

Horndon on the Hill

Many ghostly goings-on have been reported at the Bell Inn. On 26 March 1555, Thomas Higbed of Horndon House was burned to death in the courtyard of the inn for his Protestant beliefs. Guests in the Anne Boleyn Suite have reportedly woken to find a ghostly woman standing at the foot of their bed. Paranormal investigations have resulted in temperature drops being recorded, and mysterious shadows that appeared

The Worlds End public house, Tilbury. (Author's Collection)

on the wall that could only be seen through camera lenses. A wind chime began swaying in a non-existent breeze and a low murmuring was picked up on audio equipment.

People walking down the footpath at the side of the inn have reported many strange sensations: feeling extremely uneasy, shortness of breath, back pains, being choked or strangled and the feeling of someone standing behind them are just a few. A dark figure has been seen on the path and torch batteries are drained of power, before coming back to life again afterwards.

Fobbing

The Ship Inn in Fobbing has now been converted into two cottages, but the owners have reported footsteps in the attic and have heard music and sounds from the other cottages when the owners have been away. A 'Witches Bottle' was found bricked-up in the back of a fireplace in one cottage and the black liquid inside is thought to be urine, hair and fingernails of a bewitched person. The bottle is now kept at Thurrock Museum.

The Bell, Horndon on the Hill. (Author's Collection)

The Bell Inn footpath, Horndon on the Hill. (Author's Collection)

The Greyhound, Wivenhoe. (Author's Collection)

Wivenhoe

Sections of the Greyhound public house date back to the 1300s, notably the old kitchen area at the rear of the building. A poltergeist is said to cause numerous disturbances throughout the inn, including the annoying disappearance of keys. A past caretaker witnessed a plastic bag levitate above the bar floor before travelling a distance of approximately 10ft and then falling to the floor.

Staff have woken up during the night to hear the crashing of beer barrels in the cellar. As they approach, the distinct sound of a barrel being dragged across the concrete floor is heard, but when the lights are switched on, nothing has been moved. Some say the activity could be attributed to the inn's smuggling past.

The taps have been turned off, causing the pressure in the bar pumps to drop and when they have been switched back on, mischievous hands have again turned them off, much to the bar staff's frustration. Cheap perfume has also been smelt on more than one occasion without explanation.

six

TALES OF MURDER
AND SUICIDE

Thundersley

This is a most tragic tale. In 1734 a woodsman was working with a young boy in a copse at the end of Kingsley Lane on the north side of Great Common, which now runs parallel with the A127 at Rayleigh Weir. This land is adjacent to Fanton Hall Farm. The woodsman apparently became angry with the boy because of his laziness and swung his axe at him, chopping the poor lad's head clean off. In a panic, he hid the boy's body in a hollow tree in the woodland on the common. When the woodsman returned to the village he told everyone that the boy had run away because he didn't want to work. This wasn't a surprise to the locals as they all knew the boy was bone idle.

Over time, people began to hear blood-curdling screams coming from the woodland on Great Common and the woodsman was so tortured by guilt that he turned to drink, drowning his sorrows in the White Hart pub on Hart Road. The screams from the woods continued and people began to notice the woodsman's new drinking habits. Finally, he broke down in the White Hart and confessed all to the shocked drinkers. Locals say that the murdered boy's ghost would sit on the gates at the entrance to the woods and scream when anyone approached.

In more recent years some children decided to go and play in the woods, unaware of the story, and were scared witless when they saw a ghostly figure screaming out at the gates. The woodland became known locally as Shrieking Boy's Wood.

Shrieking Boy's Wood, Thundersley. (Author's Collection)

Clavering

Moat Farm was the scene of a terrible murder in 1899. The very attractive and wealthy 56-year-old Miss Camille Holland had met a kindly gentleman via a personal advertisement in a newspaper. She was swept off her feet by Herbert Samuel Douglas, but, unbeknown to her, her 55-year-old lover had recently served prison time for forgery and his first two marriages had ended when his wives both died from 'mysterious illnesses'. All Camille knew was that Herbert was an ex-army officer and had no reason to be suspicious of his past.

On 27 April 1899, the couple moved into Moat Farm, which Camille had purchased as a love nest for them. On 19 May the couple went out, but Herbert returned alone, telling the maid that Camille had gone to London and would return in a short time. The maid, 19-year-old Florence Havies, became alarmed. She had already complained to Camille about Herbert's inappropriate behaviour toward her, after he had had grabbed and tried to kiss her. For some reason Camille had not ejected her lover from Moat Farm and had managed to persuaded Florence to stay. On 16 May, three days before Miss Holland vanished, Mr Douglas had crept into the maid's bedroom; Florence yelled out for Miss Holland and an argument between the couple ensued. Miss Holland was forced to sleep with her maid for safety as tempers flared. As Miss Holland was gone, Florence did not want to be alone with Mr Douglas and fled in fear. Four years later, Herbert Samuel Douglas was finally arrested, as locals began to speculate on the whereabouts of Miss Holland. The moat was drained and Camille's body was found; Herbert had shot her and thrown her body in the lake. He was hanged on 14 July 1903.

That was when locals began to report strange goings-on at Moat Farm; a piano would be heard playing, just as Camille frequently did, although the farm was now empty. During the First World War a family experienced poltergeist activity here: doors opening and banging shut downstairs. It was reported that Herbert had apparently returned to the farm several times on the night of the murder for shots of whiskey, before finally dumping Camille's body in the moat; could the noises be a re-enactment of that fateful night at Moat Farm?

Dawes Heath

In 1917 a group of walkers were shocked to see the ghost of a woman standing next to a stile on the edge of Dawes Heath Woods, on the A129, staring blankly ahead, before vanishing. Local people tell of a heartbroken woman who was told she could not marry her sweetheart, so drowned herself in a nearby pond. She was the daughter of the farmer at Upper Wyburns Farm, which was situated on the other side of the woods.

Ashingdon

A spine-tingling cry frequently heard in the village has been blamed on a murder that took place in the lane next to St Andrew's Minster Church in Ashingdon. Two men had argued over a trivial matter, resulting in one killing the other. Plagued with remorse, the killer checked himself into a mental asylum where he died and the scream is said to be his, rather than his victim's. The lane is also said to be haunted by the cries of a woman who committed suicide by hanging herself from a tree in the lane. Her crying is said to follow passers-by for hours; even after they have left the area!

Warley

Warley Lea Farm is said to be haunted by the ghost of a bailiff who hanged himself. Loud footsteps on the stairs and unexplained bangs and clatters seem to be the main activity.

Clacton

Clacton's old 'Kinema' is now a shop, but is still reported to be haunted by the ghost of a projectionist who committed suicide after he learned that his son had been killed

The lane next to St Andrew's Minster, Ashingdon. (Author's Collection)

in action during the First World War. Staff have reported seeing an old man on the first floor and others have reported being touched by icy hands or even pushed and seeing a 'mist'. Heavy thudding footsteps are also heard, often accompanied by a slamming door.

Little Wakering

Little Wakering Hall is reputedly haunted by Betty Bury, a heartbroken woman who hanged herself in the Hall's attic after she was spurned by her lover. The bell on the roof of the Hall has been rung by unseen hands and some people have even reported seeing Betty as a headless apparition. She also is said to haunt Little Wakering Hall Lane and in the autumn she is said to glide silently from behind the church towards Wakering Wick, causing the trees to shake even though the air is still. During the late 1800s it is thought that she was responsible for continuously releasing the horses from the stables, much to the annoyance of the servants and residents.

Little Wakering Hall. (Author's Collection)

Great Wakering

Bakers Corner in Great Wakering used to be known as Baker's Grave many years ago and was a place that locals feared to pass after dusk. Legend tells of the suicide of a baker, named Clement, from Barling. He tragically hanged himself from a tree at the corner and, as was the tradition in those times, he was buried at the foot of the tree with an oak stake through the heart. This particular event gave the area the name 'Baker's Grave'.

In those days, suicides, executed 'witches' and un-christened children had little place in a churchyard. They were often buried either at their place of death, outside church walls or on the northern side of a churchyard, a place where the sun never shone. Great Wakering villagers would cower in fear on windy nights as they swore they could hear the baker's heels knocking together at the tree, as if he was still there swinging in the breeze. There are council houses built over Baker's Grave now, at the junction of Barrow Hall Road and Little Wakering Road, but years ago people said that if you ran around the tree a hundred times, the bakers ghost would appear, kneading dough!

Epping Forest

This ancient expanse of woodland bordering south-west Essex and north-east London, now has a bustling network of roads crossing it where once horse-drawn coaches trundled

Baker's Corner, Great Wakering. (Author's Collection)

along muddy tracks, constantly in fear of notorious gangs of highwaymen. One of the most famous and glamorised highwaymen of all time ruled this forest: Dick Turpin. He used the King's Oak public house, at High Beach, as a watering hole while in the forest and took the opportunity to check out potential victims to rob further into the forest.

After Turpin murdered Tom King, he fled to Yorkshire under the alias of John Palmer to lay low for a while, but he was caught out when an old schoolmaster recognised his handwriting in a letter to his brother. Turpin was arrested and held at York Castle before being publicly executed by hanging on 19 April 1739. Turpin's ghost is said to roam the Epping Forest and many people have reported seeing a cloaked, masked rider speeding through the forest. Could it be Turpin and his beloved Black Bess?

In 2003 the forest and Dick Turpin were recently a focus for a live television investigation. A paranormal investigation team attempted to catch a glimpse of Turpin's ghost by visiting the Spaniards Inn at Hampstead Heath and the Rose and Crown in Enfield, previously owned by Turpin's grandparents, which used to be an inn on the edge of the forest before housing developments shrunk the forest further into Essex. They then went on into Epping Forest from High Beech and walked towards Loughton Camp, before falling victim to one of the forests phenomena: disorientation. The crew were hit with stones, heard horses galloping and batteries mysteriously drained as 3 million viewers watched events unfold. Eventually, after an hour and a half in the forest, the crew were rescued by a forest ranger.

Another Epping Forest phenomenon occurs in a short lane that seems to be missing from all maps of the area; but after my own visit to the area, I can testify that it

The Kings Oak, High Beech. (Author's Collection)

Epping Forest. (Author's Collection)

'Hangman's Hill', Epping Forest. (Author's Collection)

definitely exists. It is only about 200 yards long and runs slightly uphill from Avey Lane onto Pynest Green Lane. If you drive your car to the Avey Lane side, put it into neutral and release the brakes, your car will roll uphill, before coming to a dead stop at a tall tree, believed to be the hanging site of an unfortunate man long ago. It is not known whether the hanging was a suicide, a murder or an official execution. This lane has been nicknamed Hangman's Hill by locals and spirit levels show a definite gradient, while other objects roll downhill onto Avey Lane, without fail, your car will roll uphill and come to a dead stop at the tree.

seven

ESSEX CASTLES

Hadleigh

Many tales of a woman wailing and crying among the ruins of Hadleigh Castle have been reported. People have also told of hearing singing and being called out to by a woman in the dead of night. Centuries ago, a milkmaid called Sally, from Castle Farm, saw a woman dressed in white walking among the ruins. The woman approached the milkmaid and requested that she return later that night. The terrified maid did not turn up that night and when she next saw the mysterious woman, she was hit around the face so hard by her that it caused permanent injury to her neck; locals cruelly nicknamed the poor girl 'Wry-Neck Sal'.

Hadleigh Castle. (Author's Collection)

Stansted Mountfitchet

Stansted Mountfitchet Castle was built by the Normans in 1066 on the site of an Iron-Age fort which had also been used by the Saxons and Vikings. The castle has gathered a reputation for paranormal activity and stories of the castle's past are blamed for the activity. Poltergeist activity here first hit the headlines in 1947, after the owners who had resided there for the previous three decades told of occurrences that had taken place while they were there. The children of the house would often be moved from their beds while they slept and pushed under tables around the house; oil lamps were blown out and locked doors would be found open with no explanation. Some airmen came to stay at the castle and all slept soundly, except for one sergeant who witnessed a floating mist that moved toward him, causing him to experience a most definite and unusual feeling.

Inner Bailey at Stanstead Mountfitchet Castle. (Author's Collection)

Outer Bailey at Stanstead Mountfitchet Castle. (Author's Collection)

The shop at Stanstead Mountfitchet Castle. (Author's Collection)

The owners of the castle flung open the doors to the public in 1985 and since then there have been a barrage of reports, ranging from strange and inexplicable occurrences to full-blown apparitions. Most of the activity seems to take place at the far end of the Armoury Room (previously the Grand Hall), within the Inner Bailey and in the office that sits above the castle shop. Footsteps, bangs and crashes have been heard by staff in the shop coming from the office above them, although, upon investigation, it proves to be empty. A man has been seen by many of the staff, standing in the doorway to the office. Objects are also frequently moved around the houses with no explanation. The sound of a flute being played has often been reported coming from the Inner Bailey and a mysterious tall figure has been seen by many visitors in the grounds of the castle. It is believed that the original twelfth-century dungeon lies undiscovered under the Armoury Room, and that bodies from the Civil War were dumped into the pit before building began.

The owners of Mountfitchet spent a year calling in electricians to solve the mysterious flickering of lights every day at midday, but no fault could be found. They have been forced to call in a vicar to try and rid the castle of the pesky spirit that seems to be tampering with the lights.

eight

THE DEVIL IN ESSEX AND TALES OF STRANGE BEASTS

Steeple

Stansgate Priory was built in the twelfth century, but the ruins of the ancient building were demolished by a landowner in 1923. Legend has it that marks in the stone walls of the building were the Devil in hiding. Centuries ago, a farmer was ploughing the field next to the old priory. The farmer was tired of the hard labour and shouted aloud that the Devil could take his soul, if only he would come and plough the fields for him. With that, the Devil appeared and snatched the plough, but the terrified farmer turned on his heels and ran towards the priory, the Devil hot on his heels. As the farmer entered the church, the Devil lunged at him, but missed and disappeared into the stone walls. Fields where the priory stood were not ploughed again until after the Second World War in fear that the Devil may reappear to claim another farmer's soul.

Runwell

Legend has it that, hundreds of years ago the rector at St Mary's Church, Father Rainaldus, was in the middle of celebrating mass, when he became possessed by the Devil. Unknown to his congregation, the priest had been dabbling in the black arts and practicing black magic. He had sold his soul to the Devil in a bizarre ritual, and now it was being claimed. Churchgoers watched in horror as the Devil himself emerged from Father Rainaldus' mouth, sending the congregation running for their

A gathering at the Running Well before it became inaccessible to the public. (Author's Collection)

lives. Some of the parishioners returned later with another priest and found a dark frothing pool of liquid with a stone face in the middle: the eyes lay hollow and the facial expression captured the sheer horror of the event to be witnessed for eternity. The stone is permanently displayed in Priory Park Museum, Southend-on-Sea.

Some locals already suspected Father Rainuldus was dabbling in Black Magic and he was known to frequently visit the 'Running Well', a deep, wide water source situated not far from the village itself. The site used to be accessed via a public footpath to the rear of a farm, behind a cluster of trees and shrubbery and down a slight hill. This same footpath carries on towards Runwell village, but in recent years the farmer who owns the land closed off the well site to the public because people were trespassing at all hours of day and night.

The well used to be on holy ground during the sixth century and was looked after by the nuns from the convent, south of the well. Legend tells of how one of the nuns, who was in charge of tending the well, was brutally raped and murdered there. Her ghostly apparition is said to still return to keep up her job of tending the well. The well itself is about 10ft across and has stone steps encircling it with a concrete platform to the side. The water level is always pretty high and slightly overflows in the winter months.

The ghost of a woman on a white horse, sitting side-saddle, has been seen a number of times near the well. A possible identification of the woman could be Epona, the Celtic Mare Goddess. Her apparition could be attracted to the Running Well because of the worship carried there, known as an Epona ritual. During the ritual, four women must be present to represent a Goddess aspect, one of the four points of the compass, a colour and a sacred site. Epona has always been connected with water, so the Running Well would be a suitable place for the ritual. The ritual allegedly builds energies at the site chosen to keep the place in a positive atmosphere.

Buckhurst Hill

The Black Shuck is a huge black 'Hound of Hell' that has terrified people across East Anglia for centuries. Trembling witnesses tell of a huge shaggy dog, much larger than an average dog and more like the size of a small horse! It is described as having flaming malevolent eyes and sometimes just one cycloptic eye which glows red or orange. Indeed, one of the most bizarre aspects of this terrifying spectre is the fact that the hound never actually attacks its victims: the dog will stalk, circle, run alongside and even confront people, snarling and foaming at the mouth, before either disappearing from sight or vanishing into thin air. Some witnesses say the dog simply walks by and ignores them completely.

Vikings first recorded sightings of the shuck. The Anglo-Saxon word *scucca* meaning 'demon' is a widely believed source of the hound's name. It is also possible that is comes from local dialect; the word 'shucky' meaning hairy or shaggy. Other names for the dog are Hellhound, Hound of Odin, and Doom Dog. It is claimed that people who see Shucks often experience a sudden death within their family or community. In more recent years the Shuck has been the basis of many fictional Hellhounds: in J.K. Rowling's book, *Harry Potter and the Prisoner of Azkaban*, the hideous black dog is called 'The Grimm', the mythical group of creatures in the *2000 AD* comic series *London Falling* have a Shuck as their leader and it is widely thought that Arthur Conan Doyles' Sherlock Homes case *The Hound of the Baskervilles* was inspired by stories of the death hound.

In 1989 a group of teenagers spotted a Black Shuck as they walked to a party through a graveyard in Buckhurst Hill. The dog was seen to cross a road and jump onto the bonnet of a passing car, alarming the driver!

Hatfield Peverel

Hatfield Peverel has a famous Devil Dog that haunted the driveway of the Shaen family residence. The Shaens lived on the land on today's B1137 road at Crix between 1770 and 1858. The dog earned the title of 'Shaen's Shaggy Dog' and although usually appearing friendly, could become extremely aggressive. The dog has not been sighted since the 1950s and locals tell of how the dog would spontaneously combust when made angry. The most famous story connected with this particular Shuck was that of a local farmer who was passing with a loaded horse-drawn wagon. The man, his horse, the wagon and the cargo were burned to ashes when the man struck out at the dog. Legend tells how the dog was last sighted spontaneously combusting after seeing a motorcar for the first time.

Thorndon

A gentleman walking along a footpath from West Horndon to Brentwood late one night in 1967 saw a big brown dog as he approached 'Horse's Pond' in Thorndon. The dog was larger than a Great Dane with eyes like fire and appeared to be stalking towards him. The dog passed by without incident, but the man was clearly shaken by the strange encounter. A week later the gentleman's brother died of a sudden heart attack and in the following August his wife, who was in her early forties, died of a brain haemorrhage.

Hawkwell

In 1965 in the village of Hawkwell, a man witnessed a huge black shaggy dog 'travel at great speed' across his garden. Two weeks later, his brother-in-law died. The B1013 in Hockley has had numerous Black Shuck sightings. A lady reported seeing the dog in 1958 as she walked alone to a bus stop. The huge shaggy dog suddenly appeared trotting alongside her, before vanishing into thin air at the bus stop. The bus-stop was on the site where the gibbet used to hang as a warning to highwaymen and smugglers. In 1991 a young couple were travelling back from a night out at the cinema, carefully driving through the bends north of Hockley, when the driver was terrified by a huge black dog, 'the size of a calf', jogging down the road in the opposite direction.

Basildon

A fascinating double tale of Black Shucks in Basildon never ceases to send shivers up the spine! Set in the 1990s, it concerns two separate locations and two separate individual stories, but both quite alarming in their own way. The first is at St Nicholas Church in the Laindon area of Basildon. This beautiful thirteenth-century timber chapel is built on a grassy hill and can be seen for miles around. Basildon district has a high population of young people and large gatherings of teenagers are not uncommon, especially in parks and quiet, uninhabited grassy areas. St Nicholas' churchyard is no exception and teens have gathered there for years to socialize.

In October 1995, a large group of about thirty teenagers were up at the church. A smaller group of females broke away from the main group and began to walk down the road away from the church. After about ten minutes the girls settled in a field and began chatting happily amongst themselves. The sun was setting, but it was still fairly light, when the girls were alarmed by the sounds of a struggle in nearby bushes. One girl described the sound as that of 'a rabbit screaming'. The girls made some brief comments on how it must be a fox killing its prey or that it was 'a werewolf'.

Just a couple of minutes later the biggest black dog any of them had ever seen appeared on the hill above them. They described the dog as being very tall, stocky and with 'huge glowing eyes'. The dog began to growl at the group and one girl took the lead in telling her friends to get up cautiously, not to turn and run, but to back away slowly. However, another girl shouted to her friends to run and hysteria ensued. When the girls reached the rest of the group at the church, no one believed them, but they were clearly distressed.

St Nicholas' Church, Laindon. (Author's Collection)

St Michael's Tower and altar as they stand today. (Author's Collection)

Inscription on the altar at St Michael's Church, Pitsea. (Author's Collection)

St Michael's Church on Pitsea Mount, which is situated to the east of Basildon district, can be viewed for miles around. Only the tower and cemetery now remain and it is no longer a place of worship, but instead houses transmitters and receivers for mobile phone signals. A group of youngsters playing in the churchyard, in approximately 1988, were witness to not one, but two black dogs. Although the dogs were described as being very large, they were not as tall as previous reports of Shuck dogs, but had the characteristic red eyes and rabid-like growling.

The dogs seemed to mirror each other in manoeuvres, mannerisms and appearance and appeared out of nowhere, snarling, slavering and threatening the youths on the north side of the church near the 'Witch's Grave'. The grave is believed to be that of a witch and she is buried on the cold, unconverted grounds on the north side of the church. The group were absolutely terrified by the dogs and even tried to climb higher to get away, but the dogs disappeared as quickly and mysteriously as they had arrived.

Hadleigh

Many Black Shuck sightings have been reported in and around the ruins of Hadleigh Castle. One group of dog walkers noticed a black dog walking in fields below and realised this was no ordinary dog when their own dogs became scared and began pulling back on their leads. When the dog below began disturbing cattle, the walkers realised that the creature was almost the same height as the cows!

Surely the most disturbing Black Shuck sighting was reported in the early 1980s by a group of children from Hadleigh. A group of youngsters had gone out on their bikes, knocking on friends' doors along the way. One girl was unable to come out until her homework was finished, so arranged to meet up with her friends later; the friends arranged to meet at the castle and rode off, laughing and chatting. When the girl had finished her homework, she set off on her bike westwards towards Hadleigh village centre and turned south into Castle Lane. She rode past all the old houses and the lane narrowed as the hill began its descent towards the castle entrance.

Suddenly, the girl noticed that her friends were coming back up the hill towards her; as they drew closer she realised they were nearly all in distress and crying. Most didn't stop to acknowledge her and flew past on their bikes, but one boy stopped to tell her what had just occurred. He said they had all set their bikes down at the south-east tower of the castle and began playing, when a huge black dog came out of the field towards them. He said it had horrible orangey-red eyes and was foaming at the mouth. They had all been absolutely terrified as it crept towards them, snarling and growling. None of the children were physically attacked but had all run screaming, after backing away from the creature.

Parents called the police and a search ensued, but no dog was found. Now the tale takes a more sinister turn: in the years following the sighting the witnesses began to meet with tragic accidents and devastating illnesses. Only the girl who was late and the boy who stopped to tell the tale survived.

Even within recent years police have been called to the castle to investigate a 'rabid' dog by numerous people on a hot summer day and found nothing but one huge paw-print in the mud!

Vange

A Black Shuck has been seen wandering from Vange towards Fobbing village near White Hall Farm. Witnesses have noted a very large black animal, the size of a pony, approximately 5ft high, but definitely with the frame and mannerisms of a dog.

Tollesbury

A lady from Tolleshunt D'Arcy told the story of how in the 1920s she used to have to cycle 2 miles to nearby Tollesbury to alert the local midwife when required. A junction called Jordan's Green on the B1023 was a place through which she loathed cycling as she knew there was a man buried there with a stake through his heart. The adjoining road was Gorwell Hall Lane (now known as The Chase) which led up northwards to Gorward Hall itself. She would always cycle through there as fast as she could.

One freezing January night after midnight, she was sent out to alert the midwife in Tollesbury. She breathed a sigh of relief as she got passed Jordan's Green, but then saw she had a gigantic dog running silently alongside her. Its head was level with her handlebars and its body appeared to be as long as her bike. She prayed the dog wouldn't knock her off her bike and said the dog was close enough to touch; she said the beast had a black, shaggy, matted coat of hair. The dog kept pace until they reached Seabrooks Lane, and then just vanished. On her return journey she was relieved that the dog didn't reappear, until she saw it lying ahead in the road sleeping at Jordan's Green. She managed to carefully navigate round the animal without waking it.

When she arrived home, she told her parents about the dog. They went out with lanterns, but the dog was gone. Her parents forbade her from travelling alone at night on that road ever again. The midwife, however, appeared to be used to encountering the Shuck and would tell how he would run alongside her bike after she had delivered babies in the local villages. The dog turned, ran alongside her one night and suddenly ran at a right angle, through the front spokes, and vanished, without knocking or upsetting the bike.

On that same road in the 1960s, a cyclist encountered the Black Shuck, one hot summer's evening. The dog appeared running alongside him, snarling and drooling. The man jumped off his bike, expecting a confrontation, but was surprised to see that the beast had vanished from sight. He told the tale of his encounter when he reached a local pub and the locals told him he was a fool to be travelling on that road alone at night!

Salcott-cum-Virley

The gamekeeper of Guisnes Court Estate in Salcott-cum-Virley was witness to the Black Shuck on a few occasions in the late 1930s. This strapping, hard-faced man admitted he and another man were scared out of their wits by a huge black dog that appeared behind their horse and cart one night on the road from Peldon towards Tolleshunt D'Arcy (B1026). The dog appeared out of nowhere as they reached the Salcott crossroads. The gamekeeper said the dog had drooping ears and its red tongue flapped out of its huge jaws, as it panted while it kept up speed behind them. He described the pitch-black dog as being as big as a calf with eyes like headlamps! The dog had vanished when they reached the estate, but the horse was sweating and shaking with fear.

Great Wakering

Great Wakering's Star Lane has a legendary black dog, reported from the time of the Norsemen, but this has somehow been confused with the Baker's Lane suicide and locals tell the story of the hound being that of the baker. Star Lane (the B1017) is named after an inn that used to sit at the side of the lane which runs between North Shoebury and Great Wakering.

Slough Hill

A creature I find most fascinating is a strange beast that is unique to Suffolk, but has often been seen crossing over the Essex border and along the Essex roads towards Saffron Walden: the Shug Monkey. The Shug Monkey is always described as being a huge, black, shaggy sheepdog, but with the face of a monkey. Sometimes he is seen running at great speed on all fours, but at other times he is seen walking on his two back legs. The best and most common place to see the Shug Monkey is a lane called Slough Hill between Balsham and West Wratting, just north of the Essex border. Drivers on the B1052 have reported seeing its huge bright eyes being lit up by their car headlights.

Other strange and mysterious creatures have been spotted in Essex, including big cats, known in the world of cryptozoology as 'ABCs' (Alien Big Cats). Hundreds of people report ABC's across the UK and even show photographic and video evidence, but none can be proven or in some cases disproved. Most cats are described as being black in colour and similar to a panther, but other reports describe a sandy-coloured lioness cat.

nine

THE WITCH COUNTY

Manningtree, Mistley and Lawford

In more recent years reports of ghost sightings in the villages of Manningtree, Mistley and Lawford have been in abundance and most either describe a male dressed uncannily like Hopkins, wretched-looking female ghosts wandering the area, or harrowing voices calling out along the shoreline naming Matthew Hopkins as their interrogator. Essex was the most notorious county for tales of witchcraft and was home to the Witchfinder General, Matthew Hopkins. Some of the most horrific and harrowing tales of witch trials and the hysteria surrounding them are from this county. There is a possibility that the pain and anguish caused by the hysteria during the Essex witch trials could be responsible for some events 'imprinting' themselves in time, resulting in hauntings and ghostly apparitions.

James or 'Cunning' Murrell was a strange gentleman who lived in a cottage in Endway, opposite St James the Less Church, in Hadleigh village. The television character who invented the talking scarecrow in the 1980s hit series *Worzel Gummidge* was based on James Murrell. He had many spells and potions that he would sell to locals to help ward off evil and was often seen gathering herbs and flowers on Hadleigh Downs and on neighbouring Canvey Island. His ghost has been spotted on many occasions, basket in hand, gathering herbs along the edges of Benfleet Creek and on Hadleigh Downs. James Murrell had an easily distinguishable face: pointy nose, high cheekbones and thin lips. When his ghost has been spotted, gathering herbs, the descriptions are uncannily similar.

In the mid-1800s, a lonely widow called Sarah Moore, lived in a tiny cottage just off Victoria Wharf. She had lost her two precious sons during a cholera epidemic; George on 12 August and John on 16 August 1850. Previously she had been known to 'cast good spells' and give herbal remedies to local pregnant women to help them through childbirth. However, after losing all that was known to her, Sarah became a spiteful, bitter drunkard. Sarah was born with a hare-lip, a crooked nose and had a twisted spine, causing her back to hunch, and now she became unhygienic, smelling like a foul creature; she had become an ugly hag.

Sarah remembered the pregnant women she had visited and resented the fact that they were blessed with healthy children. She set about making a poisonous potion, then visited each family and in turn, convincing them to give the young child a few drops of the potion. She would mutter a spell under her breath as the child drank and then began verbally abusing the family, as to why her children had died and not theirs. Within a few short weeks five children were dead as a result of Sarah's 'spell'. Parish records show the names:

> Richard Going aged 5 months – died September 4th 1850
> Mark Osbourne aged 6 months – died September 13th 1850
> Gertrude le Grys aged 2 months – died September 17th 1850
> Elizabeth Lucking aged infant – died September 24th 1850
> John Thomas Axel aged 6 weeks – died September 24th 1850

Anyone who crossed Sarah Moore's path from then on would have a curse thrown on them; some people who even looked at her the wrong way would feel her wrath. One pregnant mother of two young children was approached in the village by Sarah, who offered to tell the woman the sex of her unborn child for a small fee. The woman had no time for this and refused, but Sarah began to ridicule her for being tight with her

Seafield Bay, Manningtree. (Author's Collection)

money and that she would not only have one more mouth to feed, but two: twins! The woman smacked Sarah hard around the face when she tried to press her face up against hers and Sarah spat through gritted teeth, telling her that her babies would be born with 'my mouth', meaning her hare-lip. True enough twins arrived and they were hare-lipped! This disfigurement would remain in this woman's family for generations.

Two years later, in 1852, four children were playing in the alleyway next to Victoria Wharf, when Sarah flew out of her front door and scolded them for being too noisy. The children were 17-year-old Lizzie Hays, who was babysitting, 10-year-old Janie Hays, 12-year-old Tommy Lungly, and his 4-year-old sister Emily. After Sarah had closed her front door, the bolt hadn't been secured and the wind blew the door wide open to reveal a darkened lounge with a mysterious, bubbling cauldron inside.

The curious children crept inside to take a closer look and as Lizzie lit a candle to view the dark room they all heard the door slam and the bolt slide across. The children ran, but knocked into a flimsy wall, which caused the shelves to shake and one of the strange little bottles fell and emptied over Lizzie and Emily. Emily became distressed and Lizzie picked her up to comfort her, but then Sarah Moore flung the door open and a huge gust of wind blew in, blowing the candle flame and igniting the liquid on Lizzie and Emily's dresses. Sarah ran at them with a sack, and the terrified children ran back into the lane screaming. As Emily and Lizzie collapsed and burned to death, all the neighbours ran into the street to help. Sarah just closed her door.

Janie and Tommy were left to explain what had happened to the police constable and doctor. Janie insisted that sparks had flown from Sarah's eyes, but Tommy said it was the wind that blew the candle, a more likely tale. Janie stuck to her story, insisting until her death that sparks had flown from Sarah Moore's eyes, but there is a possibility that Janie merely saw the flame reflected in Sarah's eyes. The children both expressed terror at the fact that Sarah 'tried to catch them with her sack', but it is quite likely that Sarah just wanted to put out the blazing clothes. Parish records do indeed show two children that were burned to death on 28 February 1852: Emily Lungly aged 4 years, but also John Hays aged 17 years and 9 months, not Lizzie.

Sarah's life came to an end on 14 December 1867 (some say 1870) aged 80 years old. Legend tells of how her last spell backfired on her and killed her. Sarah would sit on Strand Wharf hoping to be paid for giving the fishermen safe passage, but one day a fisherman mocked her, asking for 'fair weather' without paying and then laughing at her. The vessel had been out on the Estuary a short time, when the skies blackened and a terrible storm broke. Lightning flashed and thunder rumbled, causing a sharp wind to blow and toss the vessel around in the water and turn her on her side. The crew shouted in terror about 'the witch' and the skipper jumped up to hack the tangled rigging, swearing and cursing Sarah's name. On the third strike of his axe, the storm ceased and the sun broke through the clouds. The terrified crew returned to Leigh to find Sarah's lifeless body slumped where she had last been seen, three huge axe gashes in her skull.

It's very likely that one of the fishermen had actually murdered Sarah with an axe because she was constantly pestering them for money. This had even made her a target for James 'Cunning' Murrell, the Hadleigh witch-doctor. Sarah was looked upon as 'a wicked witch' because she was a lonely, bitter, hare-lipped beggar with a record of horrifying tales against her name and this fact probably made the law believe she was killed by her own spell backfiring.

A drinking establishment in Elm Road, near the junction of Rectory Road, has adopted the name of this tragic woman and has her only known portrait copied onto the pub sign, which has now sadly been taken down. When the pub first opened to the public, staff and customers reported some strange activity within the pub and named Sarah as the likely culprit. Why choose her as the most likely ghost? Whenever her name was mentioned in the bar, the lights would flicker for a few seconds as if she was aware of their conversation.

Latchingdon

The Hart family lived in the village of Latchingdon in the nineteenth and twentieth centuries and were notorious witches. Legend has it that Mistress Hart had become anoyed by the bells of Latchingdon Church and one night she removed the bells from the church tower. She took them down to Burnham, where she planned to take them by boat across the River Blackwater to Wallasea Island. Unable to find a boat, she used a barrel and she used a feather as an oar. You will not be surprised to hear that she did not make the journey across the river and neither she nor the bells were ever seen again. Locals and river users tell stories of hearing the tolling of bells on stormy nights.

Strand Wharf, Old Leigh. (Author's Collection)

Canewdon

George Pickingill, was a 'cunning man' who succeeded Hadleigh's James Murrell as chief Cunning Man of Essex. He would sit outside the Anchor Inn and apparently order his 'familiars' or 'imps' to mow one of the fields at speed. His cottage was next to the pub and people would run past quickly in fear of the tiny red eyes that would stare out of the windows. These were probably the mice that lived in his home. He was said to have power over all the witches in the village and all the villagers feared him.

George's life came to a dramatic end in 1909, allegedly aged an astonishing 105 years (although parish records put him in his nineties). George was passing the churchyard on a gloomy day, when a sudden gust of wind took his hat and dropped it in the churchyard. George climbed over the wall to retrieve it, when the sun broke through the clouds above and cast the shadow of a nearby gravestone onto his face. As the cross-shaped shadow hit George's face, he died instantly. At his funeral the horses stepped out of their shafts, after delivering George's coffin to the church door, and bolted down the lane! People have reported feeling an oppressive presence around the area of the Anchor Inn and in the High Street.

The Anchor, Canewdon. (Author's Collection)

ten

COLCHESTER: THE CAPITAL OF ROMAN BRITAIN

Colchester

As Colchester is the oldest recorded town in Britain, it harbours countless tales of ghosts, witches and the paranormal. Previously named *Camulodunum* by the Romans and hailed as England's capital city, Colchester was a thriving hub of trade, import and export, until it was realised that London, with its easily navigable River Thames, would benefit the country as the new capital. Colchester still remains a very busy cultural town and is a magnet for day-trippers and tourists to flock to.

Colchester police station, in the town centre, was built on a graveyard that dates back to AD 5; this seems to be the cause of a catalogue of ghostly activity. Over the years people have noticed a presence in the ID parade room corridor, a grey phantom near a boiler room and many of the staff have been touched by unseen hands and smelt strange smells. Items have been mysteriously moved from their resting place and the ghostly presence sends chills down peoples spines. The kitchens seem particularly prone to poltergeist activity, with items moving of their own accord and other objects disappearing and reappearing in a different place.

In 1655 James Parnell, the Quaker martyr, was imprisoned at Colchester Castle after 'brawling' in Coggeshall Church. He had held a fast to pray for the sins of the Quakers and some confusion in the church led him to be arrested for blasphemy and other offences. Although he was acquitted of the charges at Chelmsford Assizes, the magistrate fined him £40. Parnell refused to pay and so was returned to the gaol.

The gaoler, Nicholas Roberts, was well known for his cruelty to prisoners and Parnell was no exception. The conditions in his cell were appalling and all efforts by local Quakers to help him were shunned by the gaoler. He was treated poorly and was forced to climb a rope to get food to eat. On one attempt, he fell and was badly injured. His health began to fail and he was unable to climb the rope to get at his food. Eventually, on 10 April 1656, after ten days unable to eat, it resulted in his tragic death. His ghost allegedly remains in the castle and haunts the dungeons.

In the 1930s a man laid a £200 bet to be locked into the castle to spend the night there. A small crowd gathered to watch the 8 p.m. lock in and it was known that he was to exit the castle the following morning at 8 a.m. Two hours later passers-by noticed someone running across the castle roof, waving their arms and shouting. The fire brigade were called and it took over an hour to get the man down off the roof. A doctor had to sedate the poor man who was described as being 'a gibbering wreck' and he was carted off to Severall's Hospital where he died a few months later, never regaining his sanity. No recent hauntings have been reported.

Hollytrees Museum and East Lodge, owned by Colchester Borough Council, are both haunted by women, but it is not clear whether the ghosts are of the same woman. Many people have assumed that the ghost is that of Miss Anne Lisle, the sister of a former Colchester apothecary, F.H. Lisle, but there seems to be little evidence that it is her, considering that the Lisles never resided in either building. I presume that people see Miss Lisle's portrait hanging in Hollytrees and have jumped to the conclusion that she is the ghost. Her portrait is described by staff as 'unusual' and almost 'creepy'.

A member of the Lodge's cleaning staff was first to report the ghost. She was alone in the building and had first of all polished some desks in the Blue Room, before heading off to the Grey Room to clean one of the carpets. It was as the woman was busy scrubbing that she first heard a 'scratching sound'; thinking it was mice, she carried on with her duties. But then she heard the distinct sound of somebody typing on a computer keyboard and the sound of the curtains swishing.

Apprehensively, the cleaner got up from the carpet and crept towards the door leading into the Blue Room. On her way, she noticed a strong perfume in the air and as she entered she had a distinct feeling of being watched. A pot of pens had been scattered across the floor, surely something she would have noticed while cleaning the desks? Then, as she turned, she came face to face with the apparition of a woman. The cleaner described her as being of slight build and wearing a grey bonnet, a crinoline dress and dainty, fingerless lace gloves. Then she vanished! The legend of the 'Grey Lady' was born. Over the years the Grey Lady has been seen by many and has been held responsible for opening doors, flicking lights and other mischievous behaviour.

Hollytrees, on the other hand, is reputedly haunted by a 'White Lady'. People have felt somebody standing behind them, usually while they gaze upon Anne Lisle's portrait and footsteps have been heard running across the floor of the Gun Room, now used as the Running-The-Home Room, although the CCTV monitors show no one in that room at the time. Large fluctuations in temperature have also been recorded; even taken by a conservator as showing 14°C throughout the museum, then rising back to normal gradually.

Colchester Castle. (Author's Collection)

Hollytrees Museum, Colchester. (Author's Collection)

Why is she called the 'White Lady'? I think it is a possible misjudgement, as the people who have caught a glimpse of her running into the Running-The-Home Room have reported 'a grey figure'. Other people are under the impression that the Hollytrees ghost is a nun.

On one occasion, when the Gun Room was opened for the day, a very strong smell of perfume wafted out. None of the staff recognised the aroma and after two days the smell had gone completely. On one occasion, a little girl visiting the museum with her family became quite distressed in the Costume Room. When she was asked what the matter was, she complained that 'she did not like the lady standing next to her daddy', but there was no lady in the room!

One afternoon, a member of staff had called his colleagues down for a cup of tea and thought he saw them both coming down the stairs and one of them turning to walk down the corridor into the kitchen. However, the second colleague then came down the stairs – so who had gone into the kitchen? When investigated, the kitchen proved to be empty, and the first member of staff said he had been alone in his descent.

Another member of staff has nicknamed the ghost as 'Lucy' and believes she is a local woman, murdered sometime in the eighteenth century. He says people have reported seeing a figure in a brown dress. Some guests have reported hearing a piano playing, but there are no pianos in the museum. Staff are now so used to the ghost of Hollytrees Museum, that they find themselves saying hello and goodbye to her each day!

BIBLIOGRAPHY

Books

Babbs, Edward, *Borley Rectory: The Final Analysis* (Six Martlets Publishing, 2003)

Banks, Ivan, *The Enigma of Borley Rectory* (Foulsham, 1996)

Benton, Philip, *History of the Rochford Hundred* (Unicorn Press, 1991)

Downes, Wesley H., *The Ghosts of Borley* (Wesley's Publications, 1993)

Jarvis, Stan, *Essex Murder Casebook* (Countryside Books, 1994)

Jones, Richard, *Haunted Britain and Ireland* (New Holland, 2007)

Payne, Jessie, *Ghost Hunters Guide to Essex* (Ian Henry Publications, 1994)

Pitt-Stanley, Sheila, *Legends of Leigh* (Ian Henry Publications, 1996)

Price, Harry, *The End of Borley Rectory* (George Harrap, 1946)

Puttick, Betty, *Ghosts of Essex* (Countryside Books, 2007)

Storey, Neil R., *A Grim Almanac of Essex* (Sutton Publishing, 2005)

Yearsley, Ian, *Hadleigh Past* (Philimore, 1998)

Websites

www.paranormaldatabase.com

www.livingtv.co.uk/mosthauntedforum

www.hauntingswebsite.com

www.forteantimes.co.uk

Other titles published by The History Press

Essex Ghost Stories
ROBERT HALLMANN

Set in the historic county of Essex, this gripping compilation includes stories of restless Vikings that still haunt their former sparring grounds; the distraught countryman of Canvey Island forever searching for his horse and cart; the mysterious haunted picture of 'Cunning' Murrell, the last witch doctor in England; and the spectre of a runaway funeral carriage.

978 0 7524 4848 0

Haunted London Underground
DAVID BRANDON & ALAN BROOKE

This chilling book reveals well-known and hitherto unpublished tales of spirits, spectres and other spooky occurrences on one of the oldest railway networks in the world. It includes the stories the ghost of an actress regularly witnessed on Aldywch station; the 'Black Nun' at Bank station; and thirteen-year-old Anne Naylor, who was murdered in 1758 near to the site of what is now Farringdon station.

978 0 7524 4746 9

Haunted London
JAMES CLARK

Drawing on historical and contemporary sources *Haunted London* contains a chilling range of ghostly phenomena. From the monk ghost who clanks his chains on Buckingham Palace's terrace every Christmas Day, the phantom horse-bus that occasionally rattles along Bayswater Road to the haunted Pig Tree, a terrifying apparition that frequents Green Park, the colourful tales featured here create a scary selection of ghostly goings-on that is bound to captivate anyone interested in the supernatural history of the area

978 0 7524 4459 8

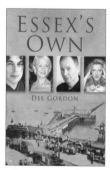

Essex's Own
DEE GORDON

Athlete and television presenter Sally Gunnell, painter Edward Bawden, actress Joan Sims, singer Billy Bragg, footballer Bobby Moore, chef Jamie Oliver, author John Fowles, film director Basil Dearden, playwright Sarah Kane, and the infamous highwayman Dick Turpin are among personalities through the ages who have been born in Essex. This book features mini-biographies of all these and many more, and will make fascinating reading for residents and visitors alike.

978 0 7509 5121 0

Visit our website and discover thousands of other History Press books.

www.thehistorypress.co.uk